YOUR GUIDE TO
RETIREMENT INCOME

JIM KRAMER

This document discusses general concepts for retirement planning, and is not intended to provide tax or legal advice. Individuals are urged to consult with their tax and legal professionals regarding these issues. This handbook should ensure that clients understand a) that annuities and some of their features have costs associated with them; b) that income received from annuities is taxable; and c) that annuities used to fund IRAs do not afford any additional measure of tax deferral for the IRA owner.

Copyright © 2014 by Gradient Positioning Systems, LLC (GPS). All rights reserved. No part of this publication may be reproduced, distributed, or transmitted in any form or by any means, electronic or mechanical, including photocopying, recording, or by any information storage and retrieval system, without written permission of the publisher, except in the case of brief quotations embodied in critical reviews and certain other noncommercial uses permitted by copyright law.

Printed in the United States of America

First Printing, 2014

Gradient Positioning Systems, LLC
4105 Lexington Avenue North, Suite 110
Arden Hills, MN 55126 (877) 901-0894

TABLE OF CONTENTS

INTRODUCTION 1

CHAPTER 1: ORGANIZE YOUR ASSETS 11

CHAPTER 2: MONEY BY COLOR 27

CHAPTER 3: HOW MUCH MONEY DO YOU NEED? 35

CHAPTER 4: SOCIAL SECURITY: THE BASICS 39

CHAPTER 5: WHAT IF SOCIAL SECURITY ISN'T ENOUGH? 55

CHAPTER 6: MAKING MONEY WITH MONEY 71

CHAPTER 7: HOW VOLATILITY CAN HURT THE INVESTOR 75

CHAPTER 8: YELLOW MONEY AND YOUR FUTURE 81

CHAPTER 9: THE BALANCED FORMULA FOR INVESTING 99

CHAPTER 10: TAX STRATEGY FOR RETIREMENT SUCCESS 103

CHAPTER 11: PREDICTING THE FUTURE OF TAXES 113

CHAPTER 12: FINDING THE FREE BRIDGE 127

CHAPTER 13: WHAT DOES LEGACY MEAN TO YOU? 135

CHAPTER 14: MAKING YOUR MARK: YOUR LEGACY 143

CHAPTER 15: HOW TO CHOOSE YOUR
FINANCIAL PROFESSIONAL 157

GLOSSARY 177

ACKNOWLEDGMENTS

Thanks to my lovely wife Karen for her support. Also, many thanks to the contributors of this book which include Nick Stovall, Mike Binger, Nate Lucius and Gradient Positioning Systems, LLC.

INTRODUCTION

Robert's father worked for the same company for nearly his entire career. He had a pension, some savings, and of course his Social Security benefits. Robert's parents paid off their house, avoided credit card debt, and enjoyed a simple but comfortable retirement.

Things are different today.

Robert has a 401(k) and an IRA, but he doesn't know what to expect from year to year. Will the market go up or down? Very few of the people he knows have a pension, and managing his personal finances seems much trickier than in his parents' day. When Robert talks to his friends and family about retirement, it seems they all share the same sentiment: things are much different today.

Money is so much more than a bank balance. It's the symbol of your time on earth: how you worked and saved, what you value, your skills and talents. Money has very practical purposes, allowing you to have shelter, food and clothing. But it also pays for your dreams. Your retirement dream is the perfect example.

You've worked hard, and now it's time to start planning that dream. The first, and most important, step in planning your retirement is knowing what YOU want. Retirement is a journey and money is the fuel that powers your adventure. Working with a financial professional: that's like hiring an expert guide.

I'm a Registered Investment Advisor and Insurance Broker, but that's just my technical title. As a Registered Investment Advisor, I have a fiduciary responsibility, which means that I'm held to a specific standard: I have a legal obligation to manage money in the best interests of my clients. But I'm more than that. I'm also your expert guide to retirement. It's my job to listen to your goals and dreams, help your create a map that gets you exactly where you want to go, and accompany you along the way to be sure there are no mishaps or detours.

What does your dream retirement look like?

Of course, you want enough money to live comfortably and maintain the lifestyle and activities you enjoy. But maybe you've also been planning to travel in your retirement or finally buy a camp for the family in the North woods. You might want to visit your grandchildren more often or pay for their college, even if you're no longer around to write the checks. With a clear idea of where you're going, we can create a map that ensures you have enough fuel (money) to get you to your destination, no matter how long your journey might be.

WHO IS JIM KRAMER?

Have you ever run into an exasperating computer problem and wished that you had a computer nerd for a friend or spouse? (Who hasn't?) Well, I'm that guy, but for finance and economics instead of computers. I've always been a problem solver, and I've gravitated toward careers that allow me to put that skill to use. Working first for the Principal Financial Group back in the '90s, and then as an independent advisor, I've seen clients through some critical times including 2001 and 2008. Along the way, I've learned some important lessons. One of those lessons is that my

INTRODUCTION

love of problem solving can actually help people. Twenty years ago, retirement planning was a whole different deal. Most people didn't need a financial planner. You invested; you increased your money. It was simple. In today's volatile, global market, an investment advisor is crucial, but finding the right one is even more crucial. As director of sales for the Principal Financial Group, I saw firsthand that there were people in the industry that weren't doing the best by their clients, people driven solely by how much money they could make.

That's when I decided to become a local advisor. My family is the reason. I have a wife, Karen, and two daughters, Kenna and Kylie, and I want to be the kind of financial professional they could count on if I weren't around. Also, I look forward to retirement myself. My wife and I have our own dreams. I know where you're coming from, and I'm excited to help you get where you're going.

IN IT FOR THE LONG HAUL

I work with people who are nearing, at or well into retirement. We can start anytime; and if you're retiring soon or already retired, the sooner the better! Ideally, I recommend meeting with an advisor when you're ten years or so away from your desired retirement age. That gives us room to work with; the more time we have, the more options will be available to you.

Ten years out from retirement, it's time to start planning your retirement, but that's just where we begin. Once we have a plan, I like to meet with my clients once a year, at least, so that we can make sure everything is on track and adjust as needed. Like I said, I'm your guide on the journey, and it's important to me to see you through. Many of my clients come to me through referrals, and that's because so many of my clients also become friends.

Like I said, I'm in it with you for the long haul. I'm a runner, and marathons are my thing. Learning to run marathons was the perfect preparation for helping my clients live their retirement dreams.

SERVICE-DRIVEN

Choosing a financial professional is probably the most important decision you'll make as you set out on this retirement journey. There's no doubt you've heard stories from friends of advisors who led them astray, put their money in risky places and lost huge chunks of their retirement savings. Perhaps you've also heard rumors about financial professionals who are simply "after your money."

It's true. As in any industry, those people are out there who won't put your best interests first. But it's equally true that many of us became financial professionals got into this business because we want to serve our clients. We consider it a huge privilege to help ensure that you get to make your retirement dreams come true. We are service-oriented financial professionals.

Here's my point: everyone who wants to retire needs a financial professional. We're not just here to work with the fabulously wealthy, and you don't need a seven-figure retirement account to come see us.

I work with many clients whose retirement savings begin below $200,000. I even serve clients who have savings closer to $100,000. If I CAN help, that's what I want to do. It's not about the commission possibilities you offer. If you go to visit with a financial professional, and that's not the sense you get, you know it's time to find someone else.

GETTING STARTED

Like I said, the sooner the better, so let's dive in. It's all about *you*: what you want, what you hope for. As you begin to think about what that might look like, here are a few things to consider:

- What are your basic income needs?

- What additional dreams – trips, vacation homes, etc. – are you looking forward to in retirement?
- What kind of legacy are you hoping to leave behind?

It's a daunting task, thinking about how to move from a regular paycheck to a highly structured income with no new money coming in. For that reason, it's not uncommon for people to avoid retirement planning … sometimes until it's too late. But let me encourage you: just get started, and you'll be surprised how fun retirement planning can be. I'm serious now. Set aside a small amount of time every day—even if it's only fifteen minutes—to organize your paperwork and accounts, or to draw up a preliminary budget. In no time at all, the overwhelming part won't seem so overwhelming anymore. Then we get to do the fun part: building a plan for your dreams.

THE BIG BOOK OF HOW

As you begin thinking about retirement, and finding a financial professional to be your guide, talk to your friends. It's always good, along the way, to share your experiences and get feedback from your friends. Talk to them about your vision for retirement, the advisors you're meeting, and the ideas you're learning about in this book. What you'll find here is a lot of information. Before you settle on a retirement plan, it's important that you prepare yourself with some general knowledge about your options, and that's what this book is about.

There is no one-size-fits-all guide to retirement. You've got options. That's one of the reasons many people avoid the subject of retirement planning, however, or keep their money in the market far too long. They're simply overwhelmed. That's also what this book is about. I'm here to take the mystery out of these complex, numerous retirement topics.

When I work with clients, I like to offer them options, educate them about the various pros and cons of each option, and then let them decide. This is *your* retirement and *your* plan. I'm just the guide. So let's get started.

BUILDING YOUR RETIREMENT

This is the basic tripping block of retirement planning: One day, your income will stop. You will no longer go to work, and you will no longer get paychecks.

I know. It sounds obvious. No more work/paycheck is the definition of retirement. How could anyone miss that? Well, they don't. What they miss is what to DO about it.

Let's imagine you're a farmer and your working life is one growing season. From the moment of the last hard freeze to the golden and amber tones of fall, you're growing and harvesting. Once winter arrives, you have to live on all of that hard work, on the food you've collected. But you don't just let that food sit in the barn, right? You freeze it and can it. You put long-lasting food in a root cellar. You dehydrate apples and make milk into cheese.

The point is this: you use all of the tools available to you to make your food last throughout the winter. If you're like my grandmother, you've become a master at this. Your food always lasts beyond the winter. You can make pies today from a crop you put up two years ago (and my Grandma was always ready to make a pie).

In retirement, you have earned all of the money you're going to earn, and it's my job to help you choose all of the right tools to preserve and extend those savings so that you always have enough, no matter how long your happy retirement journey continues.

Like my Grandma busy with her canning and freezing, retiring successfully takes work. I know, work was supposed to be finished, right? Work with the right retirement professional, and this will feel much more like planning an amazing vacation than

INTRODUCTION

work. But still, there are things that have to be done. It's not all about opening your Social Security checks. Retirement income brings thousands of complex options and accounts into your life.

If you're married, Social Security alone can be the ultimate puzzle: we run more than 20,000 different calculations to help our clients maximize their Social Security.

You must also decide how to structure other assets, including individual retirement accounts (IRAs), 401(k)s, 403(b)s, life insurance policies, and investment portfolios. My goal is to give you all of the information you need to make those decisions, and to make your decisions as simple as possible.

Like I said, there is no single path to the perfect retirement. There are many paths, many vehicles you can take and many places you can choose to visit along the way. But work with a trusted advisor, and it can be—and should be—a beautiful journey.

LET'S HIT THE ROAD

So let's get back to the beginning: your retirement dream. What does it look like? Here are some things to consider:

- What is your lifestyle now, and how much of that lifestyle do you intend to maintain? For example, right now, you might live in the four bedroom, 3,000 square-foot house you raised your three kids in, but will you continue to live there in retirement? Are you considering moving closer to your kids? Downsizing ? Moving to the beach?
- What extra expenses do you foresee in retirement? Are you hoping to travel? Buy an RV? Pay your grandkids' tuition?
- What are your priorities? If you had only one year to live, what bucket list items would you absolutely want to experience? And if you could live forever, what are some of the bigger things, like learning a new language or build your own house, would you want to accomplish?

- Who are the people most important to you? If you intend to leave a legacy, who are the people who will receive it? Who should we be considering in our planning, and what are their future needs?
- When do you hope to retire?

Once we know what your dream retirement journey looks like, we can start creating a plan to get you there. Having a good idea of your retirement dream will also help you choose the right retirement professional. We'll cover that in more depth in Chapter 14, but for now, just think of it this way: if your dream is to sail around the world, you want to hire a sailor as your guide, don't you? It's just as important to find a financial professional who can understand and connect with your retirement dreams.

The basic roadmap to retirement looks like this:

Organize your assets. Organize your finances, assets, obligations, and liabilities, and make them simple to understand. This can start with a simple list of the financial product(s) you own and a list of your debts and other obligations. A financial professional will help you sort out the value of each asset, the beneficiaries that are listed for each one, and how much risk each asset is exposed to. That last component, the risk assessment, will play a very important role in how you structure your retirement plan.

Your financial professional may also be able to help structure your plan to help you retire your debts and other obligations.

Create an income plan. The first thing you'll need on day one of your retirement is a reliable income. When your paycheck stops coming in, you still need to pay the bills. Understanding how much income you need each month and where it will come from will form the foundation for the rest of your retirement.

Accumulation. After your income needs are met, you have the opportunity to take your additional assets and leverage them for profit to provide you with income in the future, to prepare for anticipated health care costs, and to contribute to your legacy.

Taxes. Understanding how taxes affect your retirement income and accounts will help you make decisions that can save you money and protect your legacy.

Creating a Legacy. Creating a lasting legacy requires making smart financial decisions. Taking inventory of your assets with a professional will help ensure that your listed beneficiaries are up to date, that you have a strategy for covering health care costs, funeral expenses, and strategies for avoiding costly probate proceedings and tax penalties.

Finding a Financial Professional. Working with a financial services professional to craft your retirement is one of the smartest decisions you can make. The peace of mind that comes with working with someone you can trust who knows what options are available and which ones may be appropriate for you is invaluable. Choose a professional financial professional to work with who understands your needs and can connect you to the resources you need.

You will want to work with a professional who has experience in:

- IRA/401(k) rollovers
- Asset protection
- Income planning
- Wealth management
- Long-term care solutions
- Insurance
- Estate planning
- Wealth transfer strategies

The information you've read in the introduction to this book may have already changed your view on retirement. The information in the ensuing chapters can change your approach to life in retirement by giving you confidence, knowledge, and most importantly, *control* over your retirement.

This book will address your entire financial situation from four perspectives:
- Income
- Asset accumulation
- Taxes
- Legacy

1
ORGANIZE YOUR ASSETS
"Will we outlive our savings?"

That's the enduring question of retirement: Will we have enough? It sounds like it ought to be simple, but it's not. It's a question that grows more complex all the time, and you're not alone in worrying about it. One of the greatest concerns for all people planning for retirement is outliving the savings they've accumulated.

Florence and Raymond have always been dedicated savers. They had a set amount of each paycheck put into their retirement savings. They have Social Security. They even have a few insurance policies. But they both lie in bed at night, trying not to toss and turn and wake each other up or give away the fact that they can't sleep. They're sleepless for one simple reason: retirement is looming nearer and they just aren't sure if they will have enough.

Florence and Raymond are 59 and 61, respectively, and both have the happy circumstance of having their parents still alive. Florence's parents are 80 and 82, and they live in an independent retirement community a couple of hours away. Raymond's parents, 85 and 87, still live in his childhood home.

They've got great genetics on their side, but also a potentially long lifetime to pay for. And it's different for Florence and Raymond. Their parents are living on pensions.

Florence and Raymond each have a 401(k), but there's no guarantee that they've saved enough money to last the rest of their lives. They know they will both get Social Security, but neither has any idea of how much that will amount to each month. Neither of them is sure when they can retire, when they should start taking Social Security, or how much income they might need in twenty years when money isn't worth what it is now. Inflation is a huge thing keeping Florence and Raymond awake at night.

They've saved carefully, but will it be enough? Florence and Raymond keep working, and they lie in bed at night, and they hope so.

Florence and Raymond might seem woefully out of touch about their retirement, but they're in good company. Many people spend their working lives saving diligently, but that's all they know how to do. Retirement is such a large and complex issue that many people simply avoid thinking about it as long as possible.

It would be nice if a lifetime of hard work and conscientious saving could *still* ensure a comfortable retirement, as it did for past generations. But the fact is, none of us know how long we'll live, what medical issues we might face, or what unforeseen costs could be ahead of us. We could just keep saving and *hoping for the best*, but there's a much better way.

HOW WILL YOU KNOW WHEN YOU HAVE ENOUGH?

Part of the reason this is such a complicated question is actually created by some very good news: people are living longer and longer all the time. According to the Social Security Administration in 1950, men lived, on average, to age 65 and women, age 71. However, in the last half century, remarkable medical and societal advances have markedly increased lifespans. *For men and women who live to at least age 65, the average life expectancy for men is age 84 and for women is age 86* That's great news, right? And it also makes job of guessing how much retirement savings you'll need very difficult.

The end of pensions has made this question even more prevalent. Most of us remember a time when a parent or grandparent worked for one company for thirty years and then retired with a pension guaranteed to last until the end of his or her life. But as people started living longer, those pension guarantees began to wear on company's finances, making it impossible to stay competitive and support their retired workforce. One of the largest and most public failures came in 2005, when United Airlines terminated its pension program, in which more than 120,000 members stood to lose their "guaranteed" retirement plans with a total of $7.4 billion in claims.* Fortunately, in stepped the Pension Benefit Guaranty Corporation (PBGC), the government organization that insures private pension plans. But the PBGC can't absorb the costs of all failing plans, and even pensioners who receive PBGC payments don't always receive their full payments.**

All of that might sound bad, but it's not. Not with the proper planning.

What all of that really boils down to is this: now, more than ever, you really need to work with a financial specialist to retire successfully. It's still possible to make your retirement dreams come true: it just requires a new, and more specialized, set of skills.

---

*http://money.usnews.com/money/blogs/planning-to-retire/2010/08/23/the-10-biggest-failed-pension-plans

**http://www.businessweek.com/articles/2014-03-13/pension-rescue-plan-is-distasteful-yet-may-be-necessary

Today, as pensions decline, employer-sponsored 401(k) plans have taken their place. But there's even more good news: overall average retirement savings have grown in the last few decades. That's because Baby Boomers have done a great job of saving for retirement, but there's a shadow too. Younger people are not saving at the same rates, and that's something we have to turn around.*

Working with a financial advisor is a great way to make that happen as well. Families that make a practice of saving raise kids who have the saving habit too.

TEN YEARS FROM THE BIG DAY

When is it time to start working with a financial professional? While it certainly won't hurt to get advice earlier, it's a good rule of thumb to find a financial advisor you can begin meeting with about a decade from the big day.

That's because about a decade before retirement is when you need to start changing your mindset. You have to begin making the shift from the growing and harvesting phase into canning and freezing. It's time to go from accumulating to preserving, and a financial professional is equipped to offer you all of the information, strategy and tools to put you in a position of knowing you have enough for retirement.

Even if you have amassed assets like 401(k)s, IRAs and Social Security benefits, it's difficult to determine the exact amount of monthly income all of those assets will create ... and how long that will last.

A financial professional will help you structure your assets in a way that preserves the principal and protects your income, so that you know what you have and how those assets are protected,

---

*http://www.washingtonpost.com/blogs/wonkblog/wp/2013/09/03/401ks-are-replacing-pensions-thats-making-inequality-worse/

while also generating additional income for you. That way, even the mysterious future of inflation won't keep you up at night.

When you begin working with a financial professional, you'll get all of those assets in order and create a strategy for extending those assets, protecting them from market forces and safeguarding them from unnecessary penalties and taxes.

Once you have a plan, you have the power.

NEW WORLD, NEW MAP

As discussed earlier, planning for retirement has a whole new landscape. There was the era of pensions. Then came investing, and for a while, the market went up and up, and investing worked well for everyone. But today, we're in a whole new territory. The Great Recession of 2007-2008 signaled the newest phase of financial planning: the world economy.

Before the 21st century, we enjoyed a strong, growing market that was mostly influenced by financial professionals. But consider how things changed in the 90s: personal computers became prevalent and the Internet went from obscure to an everyday necessity. Thousands of people began doing their own trading on the Internet, and the numbers continue to grow. Today, people switch up their investments by the minute on their smartphones while (inadvisably) driving to work. There's more than one part of that scenario that's inadvisable, by the way. Technological advancements means that news travels very fast, and the market—which always responds to news, good and bad—can turn on a dime. A Congressional scandal could rock the market in a matter of hours, but, in today's world, even a distant event, like a riot in Eastern Europe, reaches us just as quickly as domestic disasters.

What does this mean for retirement? Does it mean investment is out? Absolutely not. It simply means that a more managed approach, particularly when you're nearing or in your retirement years, is crucial.

Another lesson of the new global economy is this: you must do MORE than invest. A secure retirement requires a strategic plan that manages your assets so that you get the most possible out of them, while also safeguarding your principle as much as possible. It's a team effort, and it requires a partner.

HOPE SO VS. KNOW SO MONEY

For most of your life, you've probably just thought of money as money. You had money you spend now and money you saved for later. But when you're making the big switch from the accumulation phase of working to the preservation stage of retirement, it can be helpful to look at money in new ways.

As you near retirement, it's important to start considering money as one of two types: *Hope So Money* and *Know So Money*. Having both kinds of money is a good thing, but what's equally important is knowing which is which. Not only will it help you make better decisions about your retirement planning, but it will

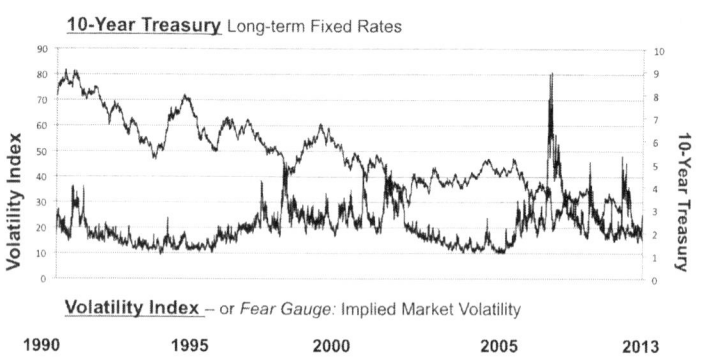

The VIX, or volatility index, of the market represents expected market volatility. When the VIX drops, economic experts expect less volatility. When the VIX rises, more volatility is expected.

also give you a greater sense of security. It will help you sleep at night, and sleeping well at night is a very important part of life, both before and after you retire.

Hope So Money is money that is at risk. It fluctuates with the market. It has no minimum guarantee. It is subject to investor activity, stock prices, market trends, buying trends, etc. You get the picture. This money is exposed to more risk but also has the potential for more reward. Because the market is subject to change, you can't really be sure what the value of your investments will be worth in the future. You can't really *rely* on it at all. For this reason, we refer to it as Hope So Money. This doesn't mean you shouldn't have some money invested in the market, but it would be dangerous to assume you can know what it will be worth in the future.

Hope So Money is an important element of a retirement plan, especially in the early stages of planning when you can trade volatility for potential returns, and when a longer investment timeframe is available to you. In the long run, time can smooth out the ups and downs of money exposed to the market. Working with a professional and leveraging a long-term investment strategy has the potential to create rewarding returns from Hope So Money.

Know So Money, on the other hand, is safer when compared to Hope So Money. Know So Money is made up of dependable, low-risk or no-risk money, and investments that you can count on. Social Security is one of the most common forms of Know

---

1. *VIX is a trademarked ticker symbol for the Chicago Board Options Exchange (CBOE) Market Volatility Index, a popular measure of the implied volatility of S&P 500 index options. Often referred to as the fear index or the fear gauge, it represents one measure of the market's expectation of stock market volatility over the next 30 day period. (wikipedia.com)*
2. *The CBOE 10-Year Treasury Note (TNX) is based on 10 times the yield-to-maturity on the most recently auctioned 10-year Treasury note.*

So Money. Income you draw or will draw from Social Security is guaranteed. You have paid into Social Security your entire career, and you can rely on that money during your retirement. Unlike the market, rates of growth for Know So Money are dependent on 10-year treasury rates. The 10-year treasury, or TNX, is commonly considered to represent a very secure and safe place for your money, hence Know So Money. The 10-year treasury drives key rates for things such as mortgage rates or CD rates. Know So Money may not be as exciting as Hope So Money, but it is safer. You can be fairly sure you will have it in the future.

Knowing the difference between Hope So and Know So Money is an important step towards a successful retirement plan. Generally speaking people who are 55 or older and who are looking ahead to retirement should start to incoporate Know So Money with Hope So Money.

Ideally, the rates of return on Hope So and Know So Money would have an overlapping area that provided an acceptable rate of risk for both types of money. In the early 1990s, interest rates were high and market volatility was low. At that time, you could invest in either Hope So or Know So Money options because the rates of return were similar from both Know So and Hope So investments, and you were likely to be fairly successful with a wide range of investment options. At that time, you could expose yourself to an acceptable amount of risk or an acceptable fixed rate. Basically, it was difficult to make a mistake during that time period. Today, you don't have those options. Market volatility is at all-time highs while interest rates are at all-time lows. They are so far apart from each other that it is hard to know what to do with your money.

Yesterday's investment rules may not work today. Not only could they hamper achieving your goals, they may actually harm your financial situation. We are currently in a period when the rates for Know So Money options are at historic lows, and the volatility of Hope So Money is higher than ever. There is no overlapping acceptable rate, making both options less than ideal. *Because of this uncertain financial landscape, wise investment strategies are more important now than ever.*

This unique situation requires fresh ideas and investment tools that haven't been relied on in the past. Investing the way your parents did will not pay off. The majority of investment ideas used by financial professionals in the 1990s aren't applicable to today's markets. That kind of investing will likely get you in trouble and compromise your retirement. Today, you need a better PLAN.

HOW MUCH RISK ARE *YOU* EXPOSED TO?

It's a scary truth, but many investors aren't even aware of the risk their money is exposed to. By dividing your money into the Hope So and Know So categories, you will start to form a better picture. First, you need to list all your assets. Next, divide them into categories using the two types of money:

Hope So Money is, as the name indicates, money that you *hope* will be there when you need it. Hope So Money represents what you would like to get out of your investments. Examples of Hope So Money include:
- Stock market funds, including index funds
- Mutual funds
- Variable annuities
- Real Estate Investment Trusts (REITS)

Know So Money is money that you know you can count on. It is safer money that isn't exposed to the level of volatility as the asset types noted above. You can more confidently count on having this money when you need it. Examples of Know So Money are:
- Government backed bonds
- Savings and checking accounts
- Fixed income annuities
- Certificates of Deposit (CDs)

- Treasuries
- Money market accounts

» *Zachary was excited when his new job offered a 401(k) with a 5 percent match. Although, with three growing kids, he wasn't able to put in much, he set up an instant transfer that would be enough to meet his company's match. Soon, he had accumulated a modest, but respectable balance. A new opportunity came along, though, and at age 58, Zachary changed jobs. He transferred his 401(k) assets into an IRA, and it was the first time he'd really thought about the account since he started it. Suddenly, he was looking at that balance in a much different way. He and his wife had always planned for him to retire at age 65, but will he have enough?*

Now Zachary has a lot of questions. Is his money exposed too much risk, since he's closing in on his possible retirement age, or should he keep it in the market so that it grows more? If he decides to move some of that money to a safer option, what investment vehicles would be safer, and how much should he move?

A RISKY QUESTION

How much risk is too much? Well, that's a complicated question with a specific and unique answer for everyone. Every person has a different level of comfort with risk, for one thing, and your financial circumstances have a huge impact on the risk question. If you have a lot of money you won't need right away (or possibly ever), it's much easier to tolerate higher risk. If you will need all of your money either now or in the near future, you might have a very different view on risk. When meeting with a financial professional, you should always understand the level of risk your money is exposed to AND be comfortable with that risk. If at any point you're uncomfortable, your advisor should help you determine a new, less risky option.

So, while risk is different for everyone, a few general considerations can help you begin to form an idea of your risk tolerance. First of all, how much money do you have, and how much of that money will you need immediately for living expenses or as liquid assets for possible emergencies?

By creating a balance of Hope So and Know So Money, you will begin to understand how much risk you can take. But how much Know So Money is enough to secure your income needs during retirement, and how much Hope So Money is enough to allow you to continue to benefit from an improving market?

In short, how do you begin to know how much risk you should be exposed to?

While there is no single approach to investment risk determination advice that is universally applicable to everyone, there are some helpful guidelines. One of the most useful is called *The Rule of 100*.

The average investor needs to accumulate assets to create a retirement plan that provides income during retirement and also allows for legacy planning. To accomplish this, they need to balance the amount of risk to which they are exposed. Risk is required because, while Know So Money is safer, more reliable and more dependable, it doesn't grow very fast, if at all. Today's historically low interest rates barely break even with current inflation. Hope So Money, while less dependable, has more potential for growth. Hope So Money can eventually become Know So Money once you move it to an investment with lower risk. Everyone's risk diversification will be different depending on their goals, age and their existing assets.

So how do you decide how much risk your assets should be exposed to? Where do you begin? Luckily, there's a guideline you can use to start making decisions about risk management. It's called the Rule of 100.

THE RULE OF 100

While there's no one formula for anyone's risk tolerance, the Rule of 100 is a rule-of-thumb kind of measure that can help you understand and shape your asset diversification.* The rule states that the number 100 minus an investor's age equals the amount of assets they should have exposed to risk.

> **The Rule of 100**: 100 - (your age) = the percentage of your assets that should be exposed to risk (Hope So Money)

For example, if you are a 30-year-old investor, the Rule of 100 would indicate that you should be focusing on investing primarily in the market and taking on a substantial amount of risk in your portfolio. The Rule of 100 suggests that 70 percent of your investments should be exposed to risk.

100 - (30 years of age) = 70 percent

Now, not every 30-year-old should have exactly 70 percent of their assets in mutual funds and stocks. The Rule of 100 is based on your chronological age, not your "financial age," which could vary based on your investment experience, your aversion or acceptance of risk and other factors. While this rule isn't an ironclad solution to anyone's finances, it's a pretty good place to start. Once you've taken the time to look at your assets with a professional to determine your risk exposure, you can use the Rule of 100 to make changes that put you in a more stable investment position — one that reflects your comfort level.

Asset Diversification disclosure – Diversification and asset allocation does not assure of guarantee better performance and cannot eliminate the risk of investment loss. Before investing, you should carefully read the applicable volatility disclosure for each of the underlying funds, which can be found in the current prospectus.

ORGANIZE YOUR ASSETS

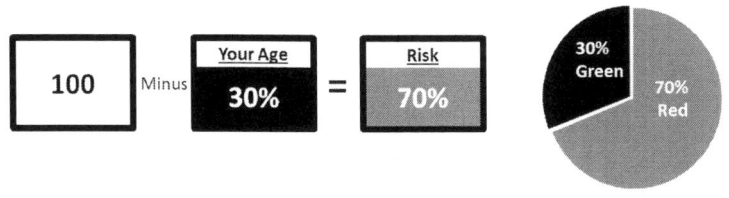

Perhaps when you were age 30 and starting your career, like in the example above, it made sense to have 70 percent of your money in the market: you had time on your side. You had plenty of time to save more money, work more and recover from a downturn in the market. Retirement was ages away, and your earning power was increasing. And indeed, younger investors should take on more risk for exactly those reasons. The potential reward of long-term involvement in the market outweighs the risk of investing when you are young.

Risk tolerance generally reduces as you get older, however. If you are 40 years old and lose 30 percent of your portfolio in a market downturn this year, you have 20 or 30 years to recover it. If you are 68 years old, you have five to 10 years (or less) to make the same recovery. That new circumstance changes your whole retirement perspective. At age 68, it's likely that you simply aren't as interested in suffering through a tough stock market. There is less time to recover from downturns, and the stakes are higher. The money you have saved is money you will soon need to provide you with income, or is money that you already need to meet your income demands.

Much of the flexibility that comes with investing earlier in life is related to *compounding*. Compounded earnings (especially on a tax-deferred basis) can be incredibly powerful over time. The longer your money has time to compound, the greater your wealth will be. This is what most people talk about when they refer to putting their money to work. This is also why the Rule of 100 favors risk for the young. If you start investing when you are young, you can invest smaller amounts of money in a more aggressive fashion because you have the potential to make a profit in a rising market and you can harness the power of compounding earnings. When you are 40, 50 or 60 years old, that potential becomes less and less and you are forced to have more money at lower amounts of risk to realize the same returns. It basically becomes more expensive to prudently invest the older you get.

You risk not having a recovery period the older you get, so should have less of your assets at risk in volatile investments. You should shift with the Rule of 100 to protect your assets and ensure that they will provide you with the income you need in retirement. Let's look at another example that illustrates how the Rule of 100 becomes more critical as you age. An 80-year-old investor who is retired and is relying on retirement assets for income, for example, needs to depend on a solid amount of Know So Money. The Rule of 100 says an 80-year-old investor should have a maximum of 20 percent of his or her assets at risk. Depending on the investor's financial position, even less risk exposure may be required. You are the only person who can make this kind of determination, but the Rule of 100 can help. Everyone has their own level of comfort. Your Rule of 100 results will be based on your values and attitudes as well as your comfort with risk.

The Rule of 100 can apply to overarching financial management and to specific investment products that you own as well. Take the 401(k) for example. Many people have them, but not many people understand how their money is allocated within their 401(k). An employer may have someone who comes in once a year and explains the models and options that employees can choose from, but that's as much guidance as most 401(k) holders get. Many 401(k) options include target date funds that change their risk exposure over time, essentially following a form of the

Rule of 100. Selecting one of these options can often be a good move for employees because they shift your risk as you age, securing more Know So Money when you need it.

A financial professional can look at your assets with you and discuss alternatives to optimize your balance between Know So and Hope So Money.

YOUR GUIDE TO RETIREMENT INCOME

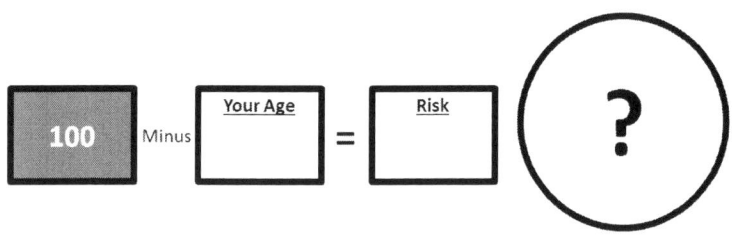

CHAPTER 1 RECAP //

- There is money you hope you'll have in the future, Hope So Money, and there's money you know you'll have in the future, Know So Money. Make sure you know how much you need when you retire.
- Organizing your assets starts with making a list. You can then understand how each asset is balanced for risk.
- Your exposure to risk is ultimately determined by you.
- Use the Rule of 100 as a general guiding principle when determining how much risk your retirement investments should be exposed to (100 - [your age] = [percentage of your investments that can comfortably exposed to risk])

2
MONEY BY COLOR

So far, we have two categories of money: Hope So and Know So. Now it's time to get even more specific and figure out how much risk each kinds of money is exposed to. That's where the colors come in.

When thinking about risk levels and money, it can help to assign colors so that you get a visual sense of the security of your total assets. Know So Money, which is safer money you can depend on, is Green Money. Hope So Money is exposed to risk and can fluctuate with the market. There are two colors of Hope So Money: Red Money, which is totally risk-exposed, and Yellow Money, which is exposed to a certain level of risk, but is managed to minimize that risk.

If you aren't sure about your level of risk, you aren't alone. That's a great reason to see a financial advisor, particularly if you're ten years or less from retirement. As you close in on the end of the accumulation phase, it becomes more and more critical that

Green Money	Red Money
"Green Money" is safer.	"Red Money" is at risk.
This is money that offers a minimum guarantee but it may pose risks other than market risk.	This is money that can go up or down in value. It may pose risk if it is not properly managed to serve a specific purpose in a comprehensive plan.

you don't lose any of the savings you've amassed. You won't be replacing them, after all.

Visually organizing your assets is an important and powerful way to get a clear picture of what kind of money you have, where it is and how you can best use it in the future. This process is as simple as listing your assets and assigning them a color based on their status as Know So or Hope So Money. Work with your financial professional to create a comprehensive inventory of your assets to understand what you are working with before making any decisions. This may be the first time you have ever sat down and sorted out all of your assets, allowing you to see how much money you have at risk in the market. Comparing the color of your investments will give you an idea of how near or far you are from adhering to the Rule of 100.

Over the course of your lifetime, it is likely that you have acquired a variety of assets. Assets can range from money that you have in a savings account or a 401(k), to a pension or an IRA. You have earned money and have made financial decisions based on the best information you had at the time. When viewed as a whole, however, you might not have an overall strategy for the management of your assets. As we have seen, it's more important than ever to know which of your assets are at risk. High market volatility and low treasury rates make for challenging financial topography. Navigating this financial landscape starts with planful asset management that takes into account your specific needs and options.

Even if you feel that you have plenty of money in your 401(k) or IRA, not knowing how much *risk* those investments are exposed to can cause you major financial suffering. Take the market crash of 2008 for example. In 2008, the average investor lost 30 percent of their 401(k). If more people had shifted their investments away from risk as they neared retirement age (i.e. the Rule of 100), they may have lost a lot less money going into retirement.

When using the Rule of 100 to calculate your level of risk, your financial age might be different than your chronological age, however. The way you organize your assets depends on your goals and your level of comfort with risk. Whatever you determine the appropriate amount of risk for you to be, you will need to organize your portfolio to reflect your goals. If you have more Red Money than Green Money, in particular, you will need to make decisions about how to move it. You can work with a financial professional to find appropriate Green Money options for your situation.

The next step is to know the right amount and ratio of Green and Red Money for you at your stage of retirement planning.

Investing heavily in Red Money and gambling all of your assets on the market is incredibly risky no matter where you fall within the Rule of 100. Money in the market can't be depended on to generate income, and a plan that leans too heavily on Red Money can easily fail, especially when investment decisions are influenced by emotional reactions to market downturns and recoveries. Not only is this an unwise plan, it can be incredibly stressful to an investor who is gambling everything on stocks and mutual funds.

But a plan that uses too much Green Money avoids all volatility and can also fail. Why? Investing all of your money in Certificates of Deposit (CDs), savings accounts, money markets and other low return accounts may provide interest and income, but that likely won't be enough to keep pace with inflation. If you focus exclusively on income from Green Money and avoid owning any stocks or mutual funds in your portfolio, you won't be able to leverage the potential for long-term growth your portfolio needs to stay healthy and productive. This is where the Rule of 100 can help you determine how much of your money should be invested in the market to anticipate your future needs.

Green Money becomes much more important as you age. While you want to reduce the amount of Red Money you have and to transition it to Green Money, you don't necessarily need all of it to generate income for you right away. Taking a closer look at Green Money, you will see there are actually different types.

NEED NOW AND NEED LATER

Money needed for income is Need Now Money. It is money you need to meet your basic needs, to pay your bills, your mortgage if you have one and the costs associated with maintaining your lifestyle. Money used for accumulation is Need Later Money. It's money that you don't need now for income, but will need to rely on down the road. Need Later Money represents income your assets will need to generate for future use. When planning your retirement, it is vital to decide how much of your assets to structure for income and how much to set aside to accumulate to create Need Later Money.

You must figure out if your income and accumulation needs are met. Your Need Now and Need Later Money are top priorities. Need Now Money, in particular, will dictate what your options for future needs are.

OPTIMIZING RISK AND FINDING THE RIGHT

BALANCE

Determining the amount of risk that is right for you depends on your specific situation. It starts by examining your particular financial position.

The Rule of 100 is a useful way to begin to deliberate the right amount of risk for you. But remember, it's just a baseline. Use it as a starting point for figuring out where your money should be. If you're a 50-year-old investor, the Rule of 100 suggests that you have 50 percent Green Money and 50 percent Red Money. Most 50-year-olds are more risk tolerant, however. There are many reasons why someone might be more risk tolerant, not the least of which is feeling young! Experienced investors, people who feel they need to gamble for a higher return, or people who have met their retirement income goals and are looking for additional ways to accumulate wealth are all candidates for investment strategies that incorporate higher levels of risk. In the end, it comes down to your personal tolerance for risk. How much are you willing to lose?

Consulting with a financial professional is often the wisest approach to calculating your risk level. A professional can help determine your risk tolerance by getting to know you, asking you a set of questions and even giving you a survey to determine your comfort level with different types of risk. Here's a typical scenario a financial professional might pose to you:

"You have $100,000 saved that you would like to invest in the market. There is an investment product that could turn your $100,000 into $120,000. That same option, however, has the potential of losing you up to $30,000, leaving you with $70,000."

Is that a scenario that you are willing to enter into? Or are you more comfortable with this one:

"You could turn your $100,000 into $110,000, but have the potential of losing $15,000, leaving you with $85,000."

Your answer to these and others types of questions will help a financial professional determine what level of risk is right for you. They can then offer you investment strategies and management plans that reflect your financial age.

THE NUMBERS DON'T LIE

When the rubber meets the road, the numbers dictate your options. Your risk tolerance is an important indicator of what kinds of investments you should consider, but if the returns from those investments don't meet your retirement goals, your income needs will likely not be met. For example, if the level of risk you are comfortable with manages your investments at a 4 percent return and you need to realize an 8 percent return, your income needs aren't going to be met when you need to rely on your investments for retirement income. A professional may encourage you to be more aggressive with your investment strategy by taking on more risk in order to give you the potential of earning a greater return. If taking more risk isn't an option that you are comfortable with, then the discussion will turn to how you can earn more money or spend less in order to align your needs with your resources more closely.

How are you going to structure your income flow during retirement? The answer to this question dictates how you determine your risk tolerance. If the numbers say that you need to be more aggressive with your investing, or that you need to modify your lifestyle, it becomes a choice you need to make.

WORKING WITH A FINANCIAL PROFESSIONAL

Take a moment to think about your income goals:

What is your lifestyle today? Would you like to maintain it into retirement? Are you meeting your needs? Are you happy with your lifestyle? What do you really *need* to live on when you retire?

Some people will have the luxury of maintaining or improving their lifestyle, while others may have to make decisions about what they need versus what they want during their retirement.

Organizing your assets, understanding the color of your money, and creating an income and accumulation plan for retirement can quickly become an overwhelming task. The fact of the matter is that financial professionals build their careers around understanding the different variables affecting retirement financing.

Working with a Registered Investment Advisor means working with a professional who is legally obligated to help you make financial decisions that are in your best interest and fall within your comfort zone. Taking steps toward creating a retirement plan is nothing to take lightly. By leveraging tax strategies, properly organizing your assets, and accumulating helpful financial products that help you meet your income and accumulation needs, you are more likely to meet your goals. You might have a million dollars socked away in a savings account, but your neighbor, who has $300,000 in a diverse investment portfolio that is tailored to their needs, may end up enjoying a better retirement lifestyle. Why? They had more than a good work ethic and a penchant for saving. They had a planful approach to retirement asset allocation.

CHAPTER 2 RECAP //

- There are two types of money: Green and Red. Green Money represents assets that are "safer" and more reliable. Red Money represents assets that are exposed to risk.
- *Need Now and Need Later.* It is important to structure your investments to provide you with income now and later.
- Working with a Registered Investment Advisor will help you compose a clear and concise inventory of your assets, and learn how much they are worth, what rules apply to them, and how they are structured for risk.
- A Registered Investment Advisor can help you structure your investments so as to reflect your risk tolerance.
- Working with an Investment Advisor means working with a professional who is legally obligated to help you make financial decisions that are in your best interest and fall within your comfort zone.

3
HOW MUCH MONEY DO YOU NEED?

Everyone has bills. At the most basic level, income is how we feed, clothe and shelter ourselves. But income needs are more complex than just basic needs. We all have a standard of living that we're accustomed to, one which most of us intend to keep (or even improve) when we're no longer working. You might enjoy eating out. You might be a member of a gym or an art museum. Once you're schedule is freed up with no more work days, perhaps you want travel to be a regular part of your life. For all of these reasons, a thorough income plan is the bedrock of a successful retirement plan.

After you have listed all of your income needs, you can begin making a plan for how to structure your finances.

Every financial strategy for retirement needs first to accommodate the day-to-day need for income. The moment your working income ceases and you start living off the money you've set aside for retirement is referred to as the retirement cliff. When you begin drawing income from your retirement assets, you have entered the distribution phase of your financial plan. **The distribution phase of your retirement plan** is when you reach the point of relying on your assets for income. On day one of your retirement, you will need a steady and reliable supply of income.

Satisfying that need for daily income entails first knowing **how much you need and when you will need it.**

How Much Money Do You Need? While this amount will be different for everyone, the general rule of thumb is that a retiree will require 70 to 80 percent of their pre-retirement income to maintain their lifestyle. Once you know what that number is, the key becomes matching your income need with the correct investment strategies, options and tools to satisfy that need.

When Do You Need Your Money? If you need income to last 10 years, use a tool that creates just that. If you need a lifetime of income, seek a tool that will do that and won't run out.

So how do you figure out how much you need and when you need it? When you take health care costs, potential emergencies, plans for moving or traveling, and other retirement expenses into account, you can really give your calculator a workout. You want to maximize retirement benefits to meet your lifetime income needs. An Investment Advisor can help you answer those questions by working with you to customize an income plan.

As we determined earlier in Chapter 1, the most important thing you need to do as you create an income plan is to take care to avoid too much exposure to risk. You can start by meeting with an Investment Advisor to organize your assets. Get your Green Money and Red Money in order and balanced to meet your needs. If the market goes down 18 percent this afternoon, you don't want that to come out of what you're relying on for next year's income. Ultimately, you have to take care of your monthly income needs to pay the bills.

CHAPTER 3 RECAP //

- The foundation of a retirement plan is detailing your income needs. That income plan will help you figure out how much money you need and when you need it, as well as how much you have to grow for later.

4

SOCIAL SECURITY: THE BASICS

Social Security is one kind of retirement income that can be considered Green Money, and at the same time, many Americans have a great deal of confusion and worries about Social Security. One thing is for sure: if you're like most of your fellow citizens, you will use Social Security as a significant portion of your retirement income. That's why one of the first steps in retirement planning is to meet with a financial professional to look at your Social Security options. And there are a lot of them. If you're married, those options are even greater.

In fact, for married couples, determining Social Security options requires more than 20,000 different calculations. That's why most financial professionals will use a computer program to analyze your unique set of circumstances. Using that program, your advisor will crunch all the numbers and then create a Social Security report, often called a Social Security Maximization Report that helps lay out a plan that ensure you receive the greatest possible lifetime benefit.

Once you have a solid idea of how much monthly income you can expect from Social Security, and at what age, you can begin building the rest of your income and retirement plan.

> » *Since the day her youngest child entered kindergarten, Candace worked as a full-time teacher. She was eligible for retirement at age 55, but didn't begin taking Social Security until 62, when she was eligible. It never occurred to her to wait any longer, but perhaps it should have.*
>
> *Last week, her grandson Harlan, now a seventh grader, asked her to help him with a report about Social Security. She was delighted! One of her favorite things about retirement was having the grandkids get off the bus at her house after school. Always an organized woman, Candace had every one of her Social Security statements filed away in the family office. She went directly to the file and pulled them out.*
>
> *That's when Candace started to wish she had helped with a school Social Security report before she retired. As she began to explain the statements to Harlan, a shocking realization began to dawn on her. She hadn't needed that Social Security income at 62. She simply took it because she thought you were supposed to file for Social Security at age 62. But now, scrutinizing these statements with her grandson, it became apparent that she was losing many thousands of dollars over her lifetime because she didn't wait a few extra years to file for her benefits.*
>
> *Could she change her mind now? A little additional school report research revealed that it was too late. She could have paid back her benefits and changed her mind for the first year only. Now the decision was permanent.*

SOCIAL SECURITY: THE BASICS

Here are some facts that illustrate how Americans currently use Social Security:
- 90 percent of Americans age 65 and older receive Social Security benefits.*
- Social Security provides 39 percent of income for retired Americans.*
- Claiming Social Security benefits at the wrong time can reduce your monthly benefit by up to 57 percent.**
- 43 percent of men and 48 percent of women claim Social Security benefits at age 62.**
- 74 percent of retirees receive reduced Social Security benefits.**
- In 2013, the average monthly Social Security benefit was $1,261. *The maximum benefit for 2013 was $2,533. The $1,272 monthly benefit reduction between the average and the maximum is applied for life.****

There are many aspects of Social Security that are well known and others that aren't. When it comes time for you to cash in on your Social Security benefit, you will have many options and choices. Social Security is a massive government program that manages retirement benefits for millions of people. Experts spend their entire careers understanding and analyzing it. Luckily, you don't have to understand all of the intricacies of Social Security to maximize its advantages. You simply need to know the best way to manage your Social Security benefit. You need to know exactly what to do to get the most from your Social Security benefit and when to do it. Taking the time to create a roadmap for your Social Security strategy will help ensure that you are able to exact your

---

*http://www.ssa.gov/pressoffice/basicfact.htm
**When to Claim Social Security Benefits, David Blanchett, CFA, CFP® January, 2013
***http://www.socialsecurity.gov/pressoffice/factsheets/colafacts2013.com

maximum benefit and efficiently coordinate it with the rest of your retirement plan.

There are many aspects of Social Security that you have no control over. You don't control how much you put into it, and you don't control what it's invested in or how the government manages it. However, you do control when and how you file for benefits. The real question about Social Security that you need to answer is, "When should I start taking Social Security?" While this is the all-important question, there are a couple of key pieces of information you need to track down first.

Before we get into a few calculations and strategies that can make all the difference, let's start by covering the basic information about Social Security which should give you an idea of where you stand. Just as the foundation of a house creates the stable platform for the rest of the framework to rest upon, your Social Security benefit is an important part of your overall retirement plan. The purpose of the information that follows is not to give an exhaustive explanation of how Social Security works, but to give you some tools and questions to start understanding how Social Security affects your retirement and how you can prepare for it.

Let's start with eligibility.

Eligibility. Understanding how and when you are eligible for Social Security benefits will help clarify what to expect when the time comes to claim them.

To receive retirement benefits from Social Security, you must earn eligibility. In almost all cases, Americans born after 1929 must earn 40 quarters of credit to be eligible to draw their Social Security retirement benefit. In 2013, a Social Security credit represents $1,160 earned in a calendar quarter. The number changes as it is indexed each year, but not drastically. In 2012, a credit represented $1,130. Four quarters of credit is the maximum number that can be earned each year. In 2013, an American would have had to earn at least $4,640 to accumulate four credits. In order to qualify for retirement benefits, you must earned a minimum number of credits. Additionally, if you are at least 62 years old and have been married to a recipient of Social Security benefits for at least 12 months, you can choose to receive Spousal Benefits. Although 40 is the minimum number of credits required to begin drawing benefits, it is important to know that once you claim your Social Security benefit, there is no going back. Although there may be cost of living adjustments made, you are locked into that base benefit amount forever.

Primary Insurance Amount. You can think of your Primary Insurance Amount (PIA) like a ripening fruit. It represents the amount of your Social Security benefit at your Full Retirement Age (FRA). Your benefit becomes fully ripe at your FRA, and will neither reduce nor increase due to early or delayed retirement options. If you opt to take benefits before your FRA, however, your monthly benefit will be less than your PIA. You will essentially be picking an unripened fruit. On the one hand, waiting until after your FRA to access your benefits will increase your benefit beyond your PIA. On the other hand, you don't want the fruit to overripen, because every month you wait is one less check you get from the government.

Full Retirement Age. Your FRA is an important figure for anyone who is planning to rely on Social Security benefits in their retirement. Depending on when you were born, there is a specific age at which you will attain FRA. Your FRA is dictated by your year of birth and is the age at which you can begin your full monthly benefit. Your FRA is important because it is half of the equation used to calculate your Social Security benefit. The other half of the equation is based on when you start taking benefits.

When Social Security was initially set up, the FRA was age 65, and it still is for people born before 1938. But as time has passed, the age for receiving full retirement benefits has increased. If you were born between 1938 and 1960, your full retirement age is somewhere on a sliding scale between 65 and 67. Anyone born in 1960 or later will now have to wait until age 67 for full benefits. Increasing the FRA has helped the government reduce the cost of the Social Security program, which pays out more than a half trillion dollars to beneficiaries every year!*

While you can begin collecting benefits as early as age 62, the amount you receive as a monthly benefit will be less than it would be if you wait until you reached your FRA or surpass your FRA. It is important to note that if you file for Social Security benefit before your FRA, *the reduction to your monthly benefit will remain in place for the rest of your life.* You can also delay receiving benefits up to age 70, in which case your benefits will be higher than your PIA for the rest of your life.

- At FRA, 100 percent of PIA is available as a monthly benefit.
- At age 62, your Social Security retirement benefits are available. For each month you take benefits prior to your FRA, however, the monthly amount of your benefit is reduced. *This reduction stays in place for the rest of your life.*
- At age 70, your monthly benefit reaches its maximum. After you turn age 70, your monthly benefit will no longer increase.

---

* http://www.ssa.gov/pressoffice/basicfact.htm

Year of birth	Full Retirement Age
1943-1954	66
1955	66 and 2 months
1956	66 and 4 months
1957	66 and 6 months
1958	66 and 8 months
1959	66 and 10 months
1960 or later	67**

ROLLING UP YOUR SOCIAL SECURITY

Your Social Security income "rolls up" the longer you wait to claim it. Your monthly benefit will continue to increase until you turn 70 years old. But because Social Security is the foundation of most people's retirement, many Americans feel that they don't have control over how or when they receive their benefits. As a matter of fact, only 4 percent of Americans wait until after their FRA to file for benefits! This trend persists, despite the fact that every dollar you increase your Social Security income by means less money you will have to spend from your nest egg to meet your retirement income needs! For many people, creating their Social Security strategy is the most important decision they can make to positively impact their retirement. *The difference between the best and worst Social Security decision can be tens of thousands of dollars over a lifetime of benefits — up to $170,000!*

Deciding NOW or LATER: Following the above logic, it makes sense to wait as long as you can to begin receiving your Social Security benefit. However, the answer isn't always that simple. Not everyone has the option of waiting. Many people need to rely on Social Security on day one of their retirement. In fact, *nearly 50 percent of 62-year-old Americans file for Social Security ben-*

** http://www.ssa.gov/OACT/progdata/nra.html

efits. Why is this number so high? Some might need the income. Others might be in poor health and don't feel they will live long enough to make FRA worthwhile for themselves or their families. It is also possible, however, that the majority of folks taking an early benefit at age 62 are simply under-informed about Social Security. Perhaps they make this major decision based on rumors and emotion.

File Immediately if You:
- Find your job is unbearable.
- Are willing to sacrifice retirement income.
- Are not healthy and need a reliable source of income.

Consider Delaying Your Benefit if You:
- Want to maximize your retirement income.
- Want to increase retirement benefits for your spouse.
- Are still working and like it.
- Are healthy and willing / able to wait to file.

So if you decide to wait, how long should you wait? Lots of people can put it off for a few years, but not everyone can wait until they are 70 years old. Your individual circumstances may be able to help you determine when you should begin taking Social Security. If you do the math, you will quickly see that between ages 62 and 70, there are 96 months in which you can file for your Social Security benefit. If you take into account those 96 months and the 96 months your spouse could also file for Social Security, the number of different strategies for structuring your benefit, you can easily end up with more than 20,000 different scenarios. It's safe to say this isn't the kind of math that most people can easily handle. Each month would result in a different benefit amount. The longer you wait, the higher your monthly benefit amount becomes. Each month you wait, however, is one less month that you receive a Social Security check.

The goal is to maximize your lifetime benefits. That may not always mean waiting until you can get the largest monthly payment. Taking the bigger picture into account, you want to find out how to get the most money out of Social Security over the number of years that you draw from it. Don't underestimate the power of optimizing your benefit: the difference between the BEST and WORST Social Security election can easily be between $30,000 to $50,000 in lifetime benefits. ***The difference can be very substantial!***

If you know that every month you wait, your Social Security benefit goes up a little bit, and you also know that every month you wait, you receive one less benefit check, how do you determine where the sweet spot is that maximizes your benefits over your lifetime? Financial professionals have access to software that will calculate the best year and month for you to file for benefits based on your default life expectancy. You can further customize that information by estimating your life expectancy based on your health, habits and family history. If you can then create an income plan (we'll get into this later in the chapter) that helps you wait until the target date for you to file for Social Security, you can optimize your retirement income strategy to get the most out of your Social Security benefit. How can you calculate your life expectancy? Well, you don't know exactly how long you'll live, but you have a better idea than the government does. They rely on averages to make their calculations. ***You have much more personal information about your health, lifestyle and family history than they do.*** You can use that knowledge to game the system and beat all the other people who are making uninformed decisions by filing early for Social Security.

While you can and should educate yourself about how Social Security works, the reality is you don't need to know a lot of general information about Social Security in order to make choices about your retirement. What you do need to know is exactly **what to do to maximize your benefit**. Because knowing what you need to do has huge impacts on your retirement! For most Americans, Social Security is the foundation of income planning for retirement. Social Security benefits represent nearly 40 percent of the income of retirees.* For many people, it can represent the largest portion of their retirement income. Not treating your Social Security benefit as an asset and investment tool can lead to sub-optimization of your largest source of retirement income.

Let's take a look at an example that shows the impact of working with a financial professional to optimize Social Security benefits:

> » *Richard and Nora Fahy met at work. Nora met Richard on her first day of work at the phone company, where he had already been a communications specialist for several years. Time passed, and they both became managers in their different departments. Things were good. They saved every chance they got, and they both participated in the company 401(k) program. Today, Richard is turning 60, so the couple decided they would celebrate—before they had dinner and a movie— by sitting down with a financial advisor recommended by some of their dearest friends.*
>
> *They visited with the advisor for a while, telling him about their kids and grandkids, and the RV they were hoping to buy to go and see all of the national parks. But the real reason they were there was to find out when that might be. They both had retirement plans, but they weren't sure how much money they would need, or how much Social Security would provide. The advisor said, No problem. Let's run a Social Security report to get a better idea of the best time to file for benefits and how much Social Security income you can expect.*

---

* *http://www.ssa.gov/pressoffice/basicfact.htm*

SOCIAL SECURITY: THE BASICS

Today Richard is 60 and Nora will be turning 58 in a couple of months. If they both file at age 62, they're looking at monthly payments of $1,900 for Richard and $900 for Nora. That would mean an estimated $492,000 in lifetime benefits. Even though that sounds like a big number, divided up over 20 years, that comes to a bit less than $25,000 each year. As a working couple, Richard and Nora live on a net income of $40,000 each year after taxes and savings.

The situation looks bleak until the advisor points something out: if each of them waits until their Full Retirement Age (FRA), they can increase their lifetime benefits to an estimated $523,700. By doing that, they can reach their Primary Insurance Amount, and that will allow them a $33,000 annual income, which is much closer to their desired lifestyle.

But then the news got even better. Because the Fahys have been diligent about saving, they won't need their Social Security income right away. They can put off filing even longer, if necessary. The advisor shows them the part of the report that defines their optimal time to begin drawing benefits, which would bring their possible lifetime benefits to $660,000! That's an increase of $148,000.

This isn't an uncommon situation, the advisor told them. I'm glad you came to see me before you filed.

That night at Richard's birthday dinner, every candle seemed to shine a little brighter.

The moral of Richard and Nora's story is this: Social Security is a complicated thing. No matter how much you think you know about your Social Security benefit, there are likely a few twists, turns and possibilities that you haven't yet uncovered. It's well worth a visit to a financial professional to ensure that you maximize this benefit you've worked for all your life.

While you might guess a call to the Social Security Administration (SSA) could answer some of these pressing questions, be warned: representatives are somewhat restricted in terms of the information they can give you, since some Social Security information can be considered election advice! As a result, the SSA trains its representatives to focus on basic monthly benefit information, rather than ways to strategize your filing timing.

MAXIMIZING YOUR LIFETIME BENEFIT

As discussed in Chapter 2, calculating how to maximize lifetime benefits is more important than waiting until age 70 for your maximum monthly benefit amount. It's about getting the most income during your lifetime. Professional benefit maximization software can target the year and month that it is most beneficial for you to file based on your life expectancy.

The three most common ages that people associate with retirement benefits are 62 (Earliest Eligible Age), 66 (Full Retirement Age), and 70 (age at which monthly maximum benefit is reached). In almost all circumstances, however, none of those three most common ages will give you the maximum lifetime benefit.

Remember, every month you wait to file, the amount of your benefit check goes up, but you also get one less check. You don't know how exactly how long you're going to live, but you have a better idea of your life expectancy than the actuaries at the Social Security Administration who can only work with averages. They can't make calculations based on your specific situation. A professional can run the numbers for you and get the target date that maximizes your potential lifetime benefits. You can't get this information from the SSA, but you *can* get it from a financial professional.

Your Social Security options don't stop here, however. There are a plethora of other choices you can make to manipulate your benefit payments.

Just a Few Types of Social Security Benefits:
- **Retired Worker Benefit.** This is the benefit with which most people are familiar. The Retired Worker Benefit is what most people are talking about when they refer to Social Security. It is your benefit based on your earnings and the amount that you have paid into the system over the span of your career.
- **Spousal Benefit.** The Spousal Benefit is available to the spouse of someone who is eligible for Retired Worker Benefits. What if there was a way for your spouse to receive his or her benefit for four years and not lose the chance to get his or her maximum benefit when he or she turns age 70? Many people do not know about this strategy and might be missing out on benefits they have earned.
- **Survivorship Benefit.** When one spouse passes away, the survivor is able to receive the larger of the two benefit amounts.
- **File and Suspend.** This concept allows for a lower-earning spouse to receive up to 50 percent of the other's PIA amount if both spouses file for benefits at the right time.
- **Restricted Application.** A higher-earning spouse may be able to start collecting a spousal benefit on the lower-earning spouse's benefit while allowing his or her benefit to continue to grow.

THE DIVORCE FACTOR

How does a divorced spouse qualify for benefits? If you have gone through a divorce, it might affect the retirement benefit to which you are entitled.

A person can receive benefits as a divorced spouse on a former spouse's Social Security record if he or she:
- Was married to the former spouse for at least 10 years;
- Is at least age 62 years old;

- Is unmarried; and
- Is not entitled to a higher Social Security benefit on his or her own record.*

With all of the different options, strategies and benefits to choose from, you can see why filing for Social Security is more complicated than just mailing in the paperwork. Gathering the data and making yourself aware of all your different options isn't enough to know exactly what to do, however. On the one hand, you can knock yourself out trying to figure out which options are best for you and wondering if you made the best decision. On the other hand, you can work with a financial professional who uses customized software that takes all the variables of your specific situation into account and calculates your best option. You have tens of thousands of different options for filing for your Social Security benefit. If your spouse is a different age than you are, it nearly doubles the amount of options you have. This is far more complicated arithmetic than most people can do on their own. If you want a truly accurate understanding of when and how to file, you need someone who will ask you the right questions about your situation, someone who has access to specialized software that can crunch the numbers. The reality is that you need to work with a professional that can provide you with the sophisticated analysis of your situation that will help you make a truly informed decision.

Important Questions about Your Social Security Benefit:
- How can I maximize my lifetime benefit? By knowing when and how to file for Social Security. This usually means waiting until you have at least reached your Full Retirement Age. A professional has the experience and the

---

*http://www.ssa.gov/retire2/yourdivspouse.htm

tools to help determine when and how you can maximize your lifetime benefits.
- Who will provide reliable advice for making these decisions? Only a professional has the tools and experience to provide you reliable advice.
- Will the Social Security Administration provide you with the advice? The Social Security Administration cannot provide you with advice or strategies for claiming your benefit. They can give you information about your monthly benefit, but that's it. They also don't have the tools to tell you what your specific best option is. They can accurately answer how the system works, but they can't advise you on what decision to make as to how and when to file for benefits.

The Maximization Report that your financial professional will generate represents an invaluable resource for understanding how and when to file for your Social Security benefit. When you get your customized Social Security Maximization Report, you will not only know all the options available to you – but you will understand the financial implications of each choice. In addition to the analysis, you will also get a report that shows *exactly* at what age – including which month and year – you should trigger benefits and how you should apply. It also includes a variety of other time-specific recommendations, such as when to apply for Medicare or take Required Minimum Distributions from your qualified plans. A report means there is no need to wonder, or to try to figure out when to take action – the Social Security Maximization Report lays it all out for you in plain English.

CHAPTER 4 RECAP //
- To get the most out of your Social Security benefit, you need to file at the right time.
- An Investment Advisor can help you determine when you should file for Social Security to get your Maximum Lifetime Benefit.

5
WHAT IF SOCIAL SECURITY ISN'T ENOUGH?

Working your whole can be seen as a long mountain climb. Once you reach the top—retirement—you get to relax and enjoy the stroll down. But since you're not working, you're not bringing in money to fuel the journey. Now you have to protect all of the fuel you worked for your entire life, and even grow some of it, if possible. Social Security will provide some of the fuel (income) for your journey down the mountain, but most people need more that just that. Social Security provides 50 percent or more of total income for 52 percent of married couples and 74 percent of unmarried persons. But let's face it: 50 percent is a long way from 100.*

---

*http://www.ssa.gov/pressoffice/basicfact.htm

So where do you turn after Social Security? Now it's time to look at your other retirement assets and potential sources of income. These include, but are certainly not limited to, pensions, IRAs, Roth IRAs, investment dividends, assets you are planning to sell, rental property, etc.

Once you have determined your Social Security monthly income and the other income you can add to that, there could still be a shortfall between that combined income and your desired income. That is called the Income Gap, and there are ways to address it.

A financial professional is the key to helping you fill that income gap using the smallest amount of capital possible. Put simply, you want to take the smallest amount of money that can be put into a yellow money tool that will generate enough money to make up that Income Gap, while still protecting your investment.

TAKING A HYBRID APPROACH TO YOUR INCOME NEEDS

You looked at Social Security strategies earlier, discovering you have some control over how and when you file. Those decisions can change the outcome of your benefit in your favor. Once you start drawing that income, it is safer and will provide you with a reliable source of income for the rest of your life. While there are many factors of Social Security that you can control, there are many that you cannot.

For example, you do not have the choice of putting more money into Social Security in order to get more out of it. If you could have the option to contribute more money toward Social Security in order to secure a guaranteed income, it would be a great way to create a Green Money asset that would enhance your retirement. Since that option isn't available, you may seek an investment tool that is similar to Social Security that provides you with a reliable income. It also has the potential to increase the value of your principal investment! This kind of win-win situation exists, and it's called an annuity.

Today, you probably have savings in a variety of assets that you acquired over the years. But you may not have taken time to examine them and assess how they will support your retirement.

It's not about whether the market goes up or down, but when it does. If it goes down at the wrong time for your five or 10 year retirement horizon, you could be in serious danger of losing some of your retirement income.

If you have assets that you would like to structure for retirement income, ***an annuity may be the right choice for you.***

Ask yourself the following questions:
- How concerned are you about finding a secure financial vehicle to protect your savings?
- How concerned are you that there may be a better way to structure your savings?

If you are concerned about the best way to fill your income gap, an income annuity investment tool is likely a good option for you. Income annuities have many similar qualities to Social Security that give them the same look and feel as that reliable benefit check you get every month. Most importantly, an income annuity can be an efficient and profitable way to solve your income gap.

HOW ANNUITIES FIT INTO AN OVERALL INCOME PLAN

Annuities are one popular and reliable type of investment tool. Annuities allow you to generate retirement income with minimal risk to your investment. In its simplest form, an annuity is a way to invest your money that allows you to structure it for income. Annuities come in a variety of modes. Finding the right one for you will take a conversation with your financial professional. Be sure you fully understand the features, benefits and costs of any annuity you are considering before investing money.

Here is how they can work:

When you put your money into an annuity, you are essentially buying an investment product from an insurance company. It is a contract between you and the insurance company that provides the investment tool. Let's say you have saved $100,000 and need it to generate income to meet your needs above and beyond your Social Security and pension checks. You give the $100,000 to an insurance company, who in turn invests it to generate growth.

They usually select investments that have modest returns over long term horizons. In other words, they generally put it somewhere stable and predictable. Most commonly, they will invest it in a combination of bonds and treasuries that are safer and dependable ways to grow money. They use the money from the insurance products they sell to invest, use a portion of the returns to generate profits for themselves, and return a portion to clients in the form of payouts, claims, and structured income options.

One of the most attractive qualities of these types of annuities is something called annual reset. Annual reset is sometimes also referred to as a "ratcheting." Instead of taking on the risk that comes with putting money in a fluctuating market, you can offset that risk onto the insurance company. It works like this: If the market goes down, you don't suffer a loss. Instead, the insurance company absorbs it. But if the market goes up, you share with the insurance company some of the profit made on the gain. The amount of gain you get is called your annuity participation rate. Typically the insurer will cap the amount of gain you can realize at somewhere between 3 and 7 percent. If the market goes up 10 percent, you would realize a portion of that gain (whatever percentage you are capped at). This means you to never lose money on your investment, while always gaining a portion of the upswings. The measurement period of your annuity can be calculated monthly, weekly and even daily, but most annuities are measured annually. The level of the index when you buy and the index level one year later will determine the amount of loss or gain. You and the insurance company are betting that the market will generally go up over time.

INCOME RIDER

When you use that $100,000 to buy a contract with an insurance company in the form of an annuity, you are pegging your money on an index. It could be the S&P 500, the Dow Jones Industrial Average or any number of indexes. To generate income from the annuity, you select something called an income rider. An income rider is a subset of an indexed annuity. Essentially, it is the amount of money from which the insurance company will pay you an income while you have your money in their annuity. Your income rider is a larger number than what your investment is actually worth, and if you select the income rider, it will increase in value over time, providing you with more income. As the insurance company holds your money and invests it, they generate a return on it that they use to pay you a regular monthly income based on a higher number. The insurance company has to outperform the amount that they pay you in order to make a profit.

Remember, insurance companies make long-term investments that provide them with predictable flows of money. They like to stabilize the amount of money that goes in and out of their doors instead of paying and receiving large unpredictable chunks at once. When you opt for an income rider, an insurance company can reliably predict how much money they will pay out to you over a set period of time. It's predictable, and they like that. They can base their business on those predictable numbers.

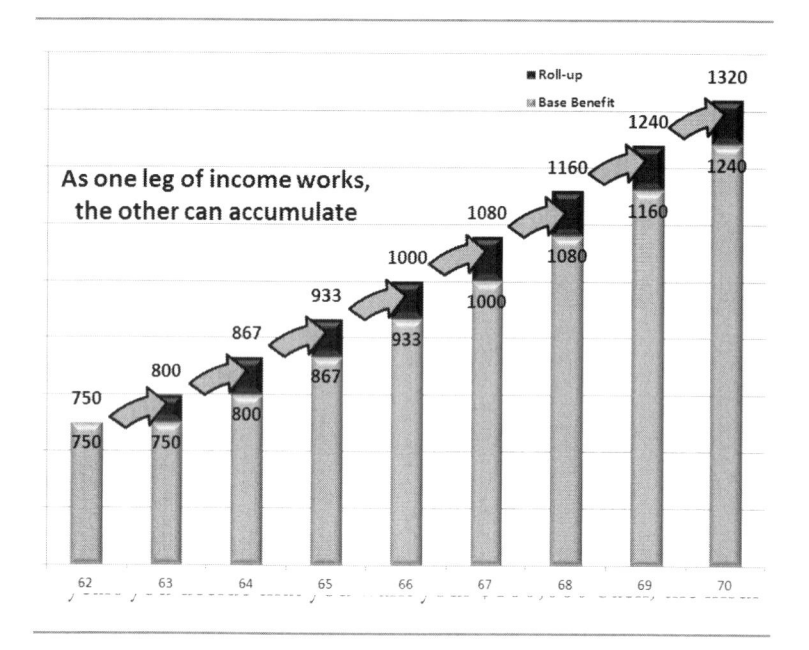

Chart: As one leg of income works, the other can accumulate

Age	Base Benefit	Roll-up
62	750	
63	750	800
64	800	867
65	867	933
66	933	1000
67	1000	1080
68	1080	1160
69	1160	1240
70	1240	1320

ance company has that money tied up in bonds and other investments with the understanding that they will have it for another seven years. Because they will take a hit on removing the money from their investments prematurely, you will have to pay a surrender charge that makes up for their loss. During the surrender period, an annuity is not a demand deposit account like a savings or checking account. The higher returns that you are guaranteed from an annuity are dependent on the timeframe you selected. The longer an insurance company can hold your money, the easier it is for them to guarantee a predictable return on it.

If you leave your money in the annuity contract, you get a reliable monthly income no matter what happens in the market. Once the surrender period has expired, you can remove your money whenever you want. Your money becomes liquid again because the insurance company has used it in an investment that fit the timeline of your surrender period. For many people, this is an attractive trade off that can provide a creative solution for filling their income gap.

When is an annuity with an income rider right for you? A good financial professional can help you make that determination by taking the time to listen closely to your situation and understanding what your needs are as you enter retirement. Every salesperson has a bag full of brochures and PowerPoint presentations, but they need to know exactly what the financial concerns of their individual clients are in order to help them make the most informed and beneficial decision. Some people need income today, others need it in five or 10 years. Others may have their income needs met but are planning to move closer to their children and will need to buy a house in 10 years. Or, if you want income in 15 years, you might want to choose a different investment product for 10 years, and then switch to an annuity with an income rider during the last five years of your timeline. Everyone's situation is different and everyone's needs are different. People who are interested in annuities, however, usually need to make decisions that affect their income needs, whether it is filling their income gap, or providing for income down the road.

What happens if you place on a shorter timeframe those assets from which you need to draw an income? Something called single premium immediate annuities may be for you:

SINGLE PREMIUM IMMEDIATE ANNUITIES (SPIA)

A single premium immediate annuity is simply a contract between you and an insurance company. SPIAs are structured so that you pay a lump sum of money (a single premium) to an insurance company, and they give you a guaranteed income over an agreed upon time period. That time period could be five years, or it could be for the remainder of your lifetime. Guarantees from insurance companies are based on the claims-paying ability of the issuing insurance company.

SPIAs provide investors with a stream of reliable income when they can't afford to take the risk of losing money in a fluctuating market. While there is general faith that the market always trends up, at least in the long-term, if you are focusing on income over a shorter period of time, you may not be able to take a big hit in the market. Beyond normal market volatility, interest rates also come with an inherent level of uncertainty, making it hard to create a dependable income on your own. SPIAs reduce risk for you by giving you regular monthly, quarterly or yearly payments that can begin the moment you buy the contract. Your financial professional can walk you through a series of different payment options to help you select the one that most closely fits your needs.

Additional Annuity Information:
- Some contracts will allow you to draw income from the high water mark that the market reaches each year. The income rider will then begin calculating its value from the high water mark.
- Variable annuities, however, can lose money with market fluctuations. As their name suggests, they vary with the market. These annuities do not take advantage of annual reset when the market goes down. The income rider will stay the same, but the value of your actual contract may fall. If you surrender the annuity, the insurance company will pay you the market value of the asset, regardless of whether it matches, exceeds or falls short of the value at which you bought the contract. If its value has dropped significantly, you may be better off taking the income rider without surrendering your contract.
- Income annuities are investment tools that look and feel a bit like Social Security. Every year you allow the money

to grow with the market, and it will "roll up" by a specific amount, paying out a specific percent to you as income each year.
- Annuities can work very well to create income, and a financial professional can help you find the one that best matches your income need, and can also structure it to work perfectly for you.

MANAGING RISK WITHIN YOUR ANNUITY

Just like any investment strategy, the amount of risk needs to fit the comfort level of the investor. Annuities are no exception. Without going into too much detail, here are some additional ways to manage risk with annuity options:
- If you want to structure an annuity investment for growth over a long period of time, you can select a variable annuity. The value of your principal investment follows the market and can lose or gain value with the market. This type of annuity can also have an income rider, but it is really more useful as an accumulation tool that bets on an improving market. A 40-year-old couple, for example, will probably want to structure more for growth and take on more risk than someone in their 70s. The 40-year-old couple may select a variable annuity with an income rider that kicks in when they plan to retire. If it rises with the market or outperforms it, the value of their investment has grown. If the market loses ground over the duration of the contract or their annuity underperforms, they can still rely on the income rider.
- If you are 68 years old and you have more immediate income needs that you need to come up with above and beyond your Social Security, you need a low risk, reliable source of income. If you choose an annuity option, you are looking for something that will pay out an income

right away over a relatively short timeframe. You probably want to consider a SPIA that pays you immediately and spans a five year period, as well as an additional annuity that begins paying you in five years, and another longer term annuity that begins paying you in 10 years. Bear in mind that each annuity contract has its own costs and fees. Review these with your financial professional before you determine the best products and strategies for your situation.

The following example shows just how helpful an indexed annuity option can be for a retiree:

> » *Allison and Lewis are both 62, and they are really ready for retirement. Allison has been a beekeeper for many years and is ready to turn more attention to her hobby, while Lewis looks at his unfinished historical novel longingly every morning before he leaves for work at 6 AM. It's a bear of a commute, and Lewis is on the road for three hours a day. Allison and Lewis decide it's time to find out exactly when their dreams can start coming true.*
>
> *They've figured out that to maintain their current lifestyle, they will need $6,000 a month. But that number doesn't take into account inflation: they have a sneaking suspicion that they will need more income as the years pass in order to maintain the same lifestyle.*
>
> *They've chosen a financial advisor who told them that their Social Security income will be $4,200 a month as a couple. They have a carriage house apartment that generates $350 each month after fees from the management company that maintains and rents it. In total, they have the potential of $4,550 in monthly income—a $1,450 Income Gap.*

WHAT IF SOCIAL SECURITY ISN'T ENOUGH?

Fortunately, Allison and Lewis have one more asset: Allison's IRA account, which now has a balance of $350,000. They also have a financial advisor they trust, which is a good thing. They might have been tempted leave the money invested in the IRA account with no management, a risky choice. Or, they could have withdrawn all of that money to put into a savings account or CD, but that would have created a huge tax liability for them.

And what's more, will that $350,000 be enough? It seems like a lot of money, but if they take $1,450 out of that account each month to make up the shortfall, it will be gone in nearly 20 years. And that doesn't even take inflation into account.

There's no way to predict future inflation exactly, but the Bureau of Labor Statistics inflation calculator* tells Allison and Lewis that what $6,000 could purchase twenty years ago would cost $9,566.52 today. If inflation keeps that pace for the next twenty years, they're going to need a lot more income.

None of the options looked very good for Allison and Lewis, but their financial professional had a suggestion: buy an indexed annuity with an income rider. They selected an annuity that was designed for their specific situation. They took the lump sum from their IRA, placed it in an indexed annuity taking advantage of annual reset so they never lost the value of their investment. In return, they got a 10 percent bonus, which would help cover inflation costs, and they were guaranteed the $1,450 of income per month that they needed to meet their retirement goals. The simplicity of the contract allowed them to do an analysis with their professional just once to understand the product. They basically put their money in an investment crockpot where they didn't have to look at it or manage it. They just needed to let it simmer.

**http://data.bls.gov/cgi-bin/cpicalc.pl*

In fact, their professional was able to find an annuity for them that allowed them their $1,450 monthly payment with a lump sum of $249,455, leaving them more than $100,000 to reinvest somewhere else. Since the annuity is in an IRA account, withdrawals are fully taxable.

» Leyla is 60 and loves her job as an art therapist for kids. She works mostly with special needs children, though, and it can be an emotionally, and sometimes physically, taxing job. She's not in a hurry to retire, but knows that it's time to start planning for the day she'll need a break. . Leyla requires $5,000 a month to maintain her current lifestyle and knows she'll need more as time goes on. After meeting with several financial planners, she chooses the one who provides her with lots of information and education. Leyla likes feeling like a partner in her retirement planning, which was a signal to her that she's found the right professional.

First, they establish that her Social Security benefit, if she begins withdrawing at 66, will provide a monthly income of $2,200. When she's 70, her pension will begin paying her an additional $1,320. It's a good start, but there's a problem: So far, Leyla has an income gap of $2,800 from age 66 to 69, and then at age 70 and after, an income gap of $1,480.

Fortunately, Leyla has a Roth IRA with a $500,000 balance. Her financial professional offers her some options.

She could use only Green Money to make up that income gap, but that would require depositing $918,360 at 2 percent to make up the gap for the rest of her life. She doesn't have that much capital, so that option won't work. Another strategy is using Red Money, withdrawing enough to cover her gap from the market. Of course, if she withdraws when the market is down, she loses principle, and she'll need big gains in the market to make up for that loss. And if a downturn *like 2000, 2008 or 2009 hits, she could potentially lose all of her safety net in a matter of just a few years. But there's a third option, a hybrid approach. Her financial profession suggested depositing $190,161 with a 2 percent return as well as buying a $146,000 income annuity. Between those two tools, Leyla's income gap is filled, and with only $336,161. What's more, Leyla can use some of the money she won't need immediately in a Yellow Money, managed investment, which will grow that money for future needs and unknown costs like inflation, medical expenses, etc. Leyla feels good about her decision, both in choosing the right advisor and finding a creative solution that will make her retirement, whenever she might take it, safe and comfortable.*

A COMPLETE INCOME PLAN

Before you retire, it's crucial that you create an income plan. A thorough income plan will help ensure that you can create a retirement strategy that allows you to maintain the lifestyle you desire for as long as you live. When you plan efficiently, you can do more than just build a comfortable, safe retirement. You can also use any Need Later Money to create a safety net for yourself or build a legacy for the people or causes you love.

Here is a basic roadmap of what we have covered so far:

- Review your income needs and look specifically at the shortfall you may have during each year of your retirement based on your Social Security income, and income from any other assets you have.
- Ask yourself where you are in your distribution phase. Is retirement one year away? 10 years away? Last year?
- Determine how much money you need and how you need to structure your existing assets to provide for that need.

- If you have an asset from which you need to generate income, consider options offered by purchasing an income rider on an annuity.

» One of the biggest challenges of retirement is understanding how much savings you'll need to generate enough income for even the most basic comfortable lifestyle. That's Gretchen's problem. She wants to retire at 68, but after meeting with a financial profession, she realizes that, even with her Social Security benefit, she will still require a minimum of $375,000 in order to generate the income she desires: $40,000 per year. Gretchen has some savings, but not enough. It becomes clear that she's going to need to make some budget changes, save more and possibly put retirement off for a year or two.

CHAPTER 5 RECAP //

- Having an income plan will help you get a picture of what your retirement is really going to look like.
- You have *Need Now Money* needs and *Need Later Money* needs. Creating an income plan is the first step toward providing for both of these needs.
- Maximizing your Social Security benefit depends on *when* and *how* you file.
- You'll need to examine your specific situation to find the best option for you.
- It's not impossible for you to calculate when the opportune time would be to trigger your Social Security income. In fact, with the tools and advice of a financial professional, it's quite easy.
- Integrating your Social Security options with the rest of your income plan will give you an idea of how much more money you need.
- Every dollar your Social Security income increases is less money you'll have to spend from your nest egg to supplement your income.
- After Social Security and your additional income is accounted for, the amount that's left to meet your needs is called the *Income Gap*.
- It is important to find ways to leverage your retirement assets to satisfy your need for lifetime income.
- It has been ages since many stocks returned meaningful dividends, so it isn't advisable to rely on them for reliable income. However, without stocks, your retirement plan will likely lose ground to inflation.
- It might be very attractive to have another asset, such as an annuity, that is designed to give you lifetime income. That income can go up in value as you wait to trigger a monthly check.

- Creating a retirement plan that focuses only on providing income will eventually have you cutting into your principle, drying it up in time and leaving you sucking up the last remaining drops.

6
MAKING MONEY WITH MONEY

So far, we've been looking at meeting your income needs, making an efficient plan as possible to generate enough for your desired lifestyle with the least amount of capital. It's no small task: understanding Social Security, figuring out other sources of income that might add to Social Security and then finding a way to fill any income gaps you might discover. That process uses your Need Now Money, but now it's time to turn to the other kid of money: Need Later.

Work with your financial professional to think about your potential future needs. With the possibility of unexpected expenses, health care needs and the always-changing issue of inflation, it's important, if possible, to grow some of your Need Later Money to cover those unknown future expenses. By investing your money wisely, you can ensure that you maintain your desired lifestyle, even if costs increase; you can also begin to think about leaving something behind, a legacy for the people and causes that have made your life meaningful.

MATH OF REBOUNDS

Anytime you lose money, it hurts. But losing money in the market can be a lot more painful than losing a wad of cash out that hole in your coat pocket. Here's why: when you lose in the market, you have to make a much greater gain just to get back to where you started.

Put simply, you invest one dollar. In the first day, you take a 50 percent loss. Now you have 50 cents. But good news! The next day, your stock makes a 50 percent gain! What do you have then? 75 cents. In order to get back to your original dollar, you actually have to make a 100 percent gain.

In a volatile market, such as the one we have now, it can become frightening to look at the large gains required just to get back to your original balance. Money is the fuel for our future, and our emotions are, naturally, very connected to our savings. That's another reason that it's important to work with a trusted financial professional when you're ready to consider investing.

HOW REAL PEOPLE MAKE INVESTMENT DECISIONS

It can be challenging to watch the stock market's erratic changes every month, week or even every day. When you have your money riding on it, the ride can feel pretty bumpy. When you are managing your money by yourself, emotions inevitably enter into the mix. The Dow Jones Industrial Average and the S&P 500 represent more to you than market fluctuations. They represent a portion of your retirement. It's hard not to be emotional about it.

Everyone knows you should buy low and sell high. But this is what is more likely to happen:

The market takes a downturn, similar to the 2008 crash, and investors see as much as a 30 percent loss in their stock holdings.

It's hard to watch, and it's harder to bear the pain of losing that much money. The math of rebounds means that they will need to rely on even larger gains just to get back to where things were before the downturn. They sell. But eventually, and inevitably, the market begins to rise again. Maybe slowly, maybe with some moderate growth, but by the time the average investor notices an upward trend and wants to buy in again, they have already missed a great deal of the gains.

An Investment Advisor will work with you to make investment recommendations based on your age, risk tolerance, and income needs. Their goal is to provide growth strategies designed to grow your money for income needs in the future.

Typically, an Investment Advisor uses professionally managed portfolios each designed with a specific objective. There are many types of portfolios available; one example is portfolios designed for immediate income to the investor. These are "need now" portfolios. Another type of portfolio might be one designed for long term growth; these are "need later" investment portfolios.

Need later investment portfolios could include a range of investment strategies from dividend stocks, to exchange traded funds, to mutual funds, and a number of other strategies. Need later money typically can afford to have some volatility since the investor is not tapping into the funds at the present time.

In my opinion, a good Investment Advisor should be cautious from the outset to select investment options that the investor is comfortable with. A risk tolerance questionnaire, completed by the investor allows the Advisor to learn how the client may react to both positive and negative market events.

I believe that the stock market will be highly volatile for years to come. I feel global economic events, government debt, as well as the explosion of Internet day trading have all contributed to this volatility.

Normally, the more the volatile the investment portfolio is, the greater growth potential. The investor needs to fully understand the risk level of the portfolios the Advisor is recommending before investing. A risk adverse investor might consider using a variable or fixed indexed annuity with an income rider. If the market does well, the investor benefits from the growth (although perhaps not as well as a well-managed need later investment portfolio). However, if the market fails to perform well, the investor can lean on the income benefits of an annuity and the guarantees that it can provide. It is imperative that the investor and Advisor be on the same page before initiating a strategy. Communication is vital.

It is important to note that annuities are designed to be long-term investments and frequently involve substantial charges such as administrative fees, annual contract fees, mortality & risk expense charges and surrender charges. Early withdrawals may impact annuity cash values and death benefits. Taxes are payable upon withdrawal of funds. An additional 10% IRS penalty may apply to withdrawals prior to age 59 ½. Annuities are not guaranteed by FDIC or any other governmental agency and are not deposits or other obligations of, or guaranteed or endorsed by any bank or savings association. With fixed annuities, both the money you invest and the interest paid out are guaranteed by the claims-paying ability of the insurer. Investments in variable annuities will fluctuate and values upon redemption may be less than the original amount invested. Investors should consider the investment objectives, risks, charges, and expenses of a fixed/variable annuity carefully before investing. Prospectuses containing this and other information about the annuity are available by contacting your investment advisor. Please read the prospectus carefully before investing to ensure the fixed/variable annuity is appropriate for your goals and risk tolerance.

7
HOW VOLATILITY CAN HURT THE INVESTOR

» *Eva is in a difficult situation. She has had a steady, excellent job for 34 years at a manufacturing company. During her time there, she always had great work reviews, which resulted in promotions, bonuses and pay raises that included company stock. She also participates in her company's 401(k) program using a portion of her paycheck to buy Acme stock. She feels great about all of the investments she's been putting away, but she doesn't know much about managing those assets. By the time she retires, Eva is the proud owner of $250,000 in her company's stock.*

Then an unexpected problem occurs. Eva develops an illness that requires ongoing treatment. Between doctor visits and the exhaustion created by the treatment, Eva begins to do poorly at work. Her employers are supportive, but it soon becomes clear that retirement is the only way Eva can get enough rest to continue her treatment. A week after her 62nd birthday, Eva's colleagues throw her a huge retirement, and she gets set to start a new, hopefully healthier, part of her life.

Eva's only retirement income is her company stock, so when she retires, she has to begin taking Social Security immediately. That means taking a lower payment, but it's Eva's only option. She will receive a $1,900 monthly Social Security payment, but that only gets her part way to her $3,500 monthly income needs.

Eva decides to sell $1,600 of her company stock every month to cover her income gap. But that's a frightening strategy: by removing $1,600 of her principle every month, Eva is losing her nest egg quickly. And that's just if the market is stable or slightly increasing. What if a market downturn hits, and Eva loses 30 percent or more of her only retirement savings? She will have to make even larger gains just to get back to zero.

Sadly, Eva's retirement coincides with the market downturn in 2008. She sustains a major loss of 20 percent, which is never a good time to remove money from your principle. But Eva has no other choice; she needs to pay her bills. She continues to sell stock every time she needs money, which isn't an unusual occasion, since is still dealing with health problems. Eventually, as the stock price continues to drop, she has to sell more and more stock just to make enough money to meet her income needs.

Too late, a friend tells Eva that she could have restructured her investment into a tool that would have protected her balance and delivered her an income. Had she known, or had she consulted a financial professional, she might have been able to keep her $250,000 as well as protect her assets from increasing income costs. Eva didn't know about money colors,

HOW VOLATILITY CAN HURT THE INVESTOR

but it's clear now that her Red Money risk hurt her retirement dreams.

In 2013, DALBAR, the well-respected financial services market research firm, released their annual "Quantitative Analysis of Investment Behavior" report (QAIB). The report studied the impact of market volatility on individual investors: people like Lisa, or anyone who was managing (or mismanaging) their own investments in the stock market.

According to the study, volatility not only caused investors to make decisions based on their emotions, those decisions also harmed their investments and prevented them from realizing potential gains. So why do people meddle so much with their investments when the market is fluctuating? Part of the reason is that many people have financial obligations that they don't have control over. Significant expenses like house payments, the unexpected cost of replacing a broken-down car, and medical bills can put people in a position where they need money. If they need to sell investments to come up with that money, they don't have the luxury of selling when they *want* to. They must sell when they *need* to.

DALBAR's "Quantitative Analysis of Investor Behavior" has been used to measure the effects of investors' buying, selling and mutual fund switching decisions since 1994. The QAIB shows time and time again over nearly a 20 year period that the average investor earns less, and in many cases, significantly less than the performance of mutual funds suggests. QAIB's goal is to improve independent investor performance and to help financial professionals provide helpful advice and investment strategies that address the concerns and behaviors of the average investor.

An excerpt from the report claims that:

"QAIB offers guidance on how and where investor behaviors can be improved. No matter what the state of the mutual fund industry,

boom or bust: Investment results are more dependent on investor behavior than on fund performance. Mutual fund investors who hold on to their investments are more successful than those who time the market.

QAIB uses data from the Investment Company Institute (ICI), Standard & Poor's and Barclays

Capital Index Products to compare mutual fund investor returns to an appropriate set of benchmarks.

There are actually three primary causes for the chronic shortfall for both equity and fixed income investors:

1. *Capital not available to invest. This accounts for 25 percent to 35 percent of the shortfall*
2. *Capital needed for other purposes. This accounts for 35 percent to 45 percent of the shortfall.*
3. *Psychological factors. These account for 45 percent to 55 percent of the shortfall."*

The key findings of Dalbar's QAIB report provide compelling statistics about how individual investment strategies produced negative outcomes for the majority of investors:

- Psychological factors account for 45 percent to 55 percent of the chronic investment return shortfall for both equity and fixed income investors.
- Asset allocation is designed to handle the investment decision-making for the investor, which can materially reduce the shortfall due to psychological factors.
- Successful asset allocation investing requires investors to act on two critical imperatives:
  a. Balance capital preservation and appreciation so that they are aligned with the investor's objective.
  b. Select a qualified allocator.
- The best way for an investor to determine their risk tolerance is to utilize a risk tolerance assessment. However, these assessments must be accessible and usable.

- Evaluating allocator quality requires analysis of the allocator's underlying investments, decision making process and whether or not past efforts have produced successful outcomes.
- Choosing a top allocator makes a significant difference in the investment results one will achieve.
- Mutual fund retention rates suggest that the average investor has not remained invested for long enough periods to derive the potential benefits of the investment markets.
- Retention rates for asset allocation funds exceed those of equity and fixed income funds by over a year.
- Investors' ability to correctly time the market is highly dependent on the direction of the market. Investors generally guess right more often in up markets. However, in 2012 investors guessed right only 42 percent of the time during a bull market.
- Analysis of investor fund flows compared to market performance further supports the argument that investors are unsuccessful at timing the market. Market upswings rarely coincide with mutual fund inflows while market downturns do not coincide with mutual fund outflows.
- Average equity mutual fund investors gained 15.56 percent compared to a gain of 15.98 percent that just holding the S&P 500 produced.
- The shortfall in the long-term annualized return of the average mutual fund equity investor and the S&P 500 continued to decrease in 2012.
- The fixed-income investor experienced a return of 4.68 percent compared to an advance of 4.21 percent on the Barclays Aggregate Bond Index.
- The average fixed income investor has failed to keep up with inflation in nine out of the last 14 years.*

---

*2013 QAIB, Dalbar, March 2013

It doesn't take a financial services market research report to tell you that market volatility is out of your control. The report does prove, however, that before you experience market volatility, you should have an investment plan, and when the market is fluctuating, you should stand by your investment plan. You should also review and discuss your investment plan with your financial professional on a regular basis, ensuring he/she is aware of any changes in your goals, financial circumstances, your health or your risk tolerance. When the economy is under stress and the markets are volatile, investors can feel vulnerable. That vulnerability causes people to tinker with their portfolios in an attempt to outsmart the market. Financial professionals, however, don't try to time the market for their clients. They try to tap into the gains that can be realized by committing to long-term investment strategies.

8
YELLOW MONEY AND YOUR FUTURE

Now that you've calculated the Rule of 100, determined how much risk you have and how much you want, and you've determined how much Green Money you need to meet your short-term and mid-term income needs, it's time to look at what you have left. The money you have left after you've calculated your Green Money needs has the potential of becoming Red Money: your stocks, mutual funds and other investment products that you want to continue accumulating value with the market. You now have the luxury of taking a closer second look at your Red Money to determine how you would like to manage it.

As you read earlier in the key findings of the DALBAR report, the deck is stacked against the individual investor. Remember that the average investor on a fixed income failed to keep pace with inflation in nine of the last 14 years, meaning the inherent risk in managing your Red Money is very real and could have a lasting impact on your assets. So, how much of your Red Money do you invest, and in what kinds of markets, investment products and stocks do you invest? There are a lot of different directions in which you can take your Red Money. One thing is for sure: significant accumulation depends on investing in the market. How you go about doing it is different for everyone. Gathering stocks, bonds and investment funds together in a portfolio without a cohesive strategy behind them could cause you to miss out on the benefits of a more thoughtful and planful approach. The end result is that you may never really understand what your money is doing, where and how it is really invested, and which investment principles are behind the investment products you hold. While you may have goals for each individual piece of your portfolio, it is likely that you don't have a comprehensive plan for your Red Money, which may mean that *you are taking on more risk than you would like, and are getting less return for it than is possible.*

Enter **Yellow Money**. Yellow Money is money that is managed by a professional *with a purpose*. Yellow money is generally recommended for accumulation purposes but can also be used to cover current income needs as an alternative or in combination with Green Money. Low volatility portfolios such as a Laddered Income approach can be used to assist with your income needs. In fact, Yellow Money strategies can deliver even higher income than Green Money. The problem is that it is not as consistent as Green Money and is subject to a degree of volatility. The best purpose of Yellow Money is for long term growth accumulation.

After your income needs are met and you have assets that you would like to dedicate to accumulation, there are decisions you need to make about how to invest those assets. You can buy stocks, index funds, mutual funds, bonds — you name it — you can invest in it. However, the difference between Red Money and Yellow Money is that Yellow Money has a cohesive strategy behind it that is *implemented by a professiona*l. When you manage your

Red Money with an investment plan, it becomes Yellow Money: *money that is being managed with a specific purpose, a specific set of focused goals and a specific strategy in mind.* Yellow Money is still a type of Red Money. It comes with different levels of risk. But Yellow Money is under the watchful eye of professionals who have a stake in the success of your money in the market and who can recommend a range of strategies from those designed for preservation to those targeting rapid growth. You don't want to miss out on achieving the right level of risk, and more importantly, composing a careful plan for the return of your assets.

It can be helpful to think of Red Money and Yellow Money with this analogy:

If you needed to travel through an unfamiliar city in a foreign country, you could rent a car or perhaps hire a driver. Were you to drive yourself, you would try to gain guidance from perplexing road signs and need to adhere to traffic rules – with no experience or assistance to lean on. It would take longer to get to where you want to go, and the chance of a traffic accident would be higher. If you hired a driver, they would manage your journey. A driver would know the route, how to avoid traffic, and follow the rules of the road.

Red Money is like driving yourself. With Yellow Money, you are still traveling by car, but now you have a professional working on your behalf.

TAKING A CLOSER LOOK AT YOUR PORTFOLIO

Think about your investment portfolio. Think specifically of what you would consider your Red Money. Do you know what is there? You may have several different investment products like individual mutual funds, bond accounts, stocks, etc. You may have inherited a stock portfolio from a relative, or you might be invested in a bond account offered by the company for which you worked due to your familiarity with them. While you may or may not be managing your investments individually, the reality is that you probably don't have an overall management strategy for all of your investments. Investments that aren't managed are simply Red Money, or money that is at risk in the market.

Harnessing the earning potential of your Red Money relies on more than a collection of stocks and bonds, however. It needs guided management. A good Yellow Money manager uses the knowledge they have about the level of risk with which you are comfortable, what you need or want to use your money for, when you want or need it and how you want to use it. The Yellow Money objects that they choose for you will still have a certain level of risk, but under the right management, control and process, you have a far better chance of a successful outcome that meets your specific needs.

When you sit down with an investment professional, you can look at all of your assets together. Chances are that you have accumulated a number of different assets over the last 20, 30 or 50 years. You may have a 401(k), an IRA, a Roth IRA, an account of self-directed stocks, a brokerage account, etc. Wherever you put your money, a financial professional will go through your assets and help you determine the level of risk to which you are exposed now and should be exposed in the future.

Here is a typical example of how an investment professional can be helpful to a future retiree with Yellow Money needs:

> » *Gabriel and Rebecca came to see me several years ago. They were both 60 and hoping to retire, but they were already nervous that they didn't have enough savings. Gabriel is a pastor. His wife doesn't officially work, although being a pastor's wife is certainly more than a 40-hour-a-week responsibility. Her church duties, which she loved, made it impossible for her to take on another job. But that also meant that Gabriel and Rebecca hadn't been able to save as much as they had hoped.*

When they came to see me, they had a Roth IRA with just under $100,000 in it. They owned a few insurance policies and their house, but they aren't sure how much their assets would amount to as retirement income. We visit for a while, and I asked them a few questions.

1. Do you know exactly where all of you money is? *They do. Because they've only been able to save a little, they stuck with one retirement account.*

2. Do they know what types of assets they own? *Sort of ... Gabriel set up their IRA online, and he is the one who makes the deposits into it. And yet, neither Gabriel and Rebecca knows exactly what their IRA portfolio Investments are. What's more, they're both hoping to retire in 5 years, and neither of them is aware that their very small nest egg is sitting at risk right now.*

3. Do they know the strategies behind each one of the investment products they own? *Neither Rebecca or Gabriel knows what their IRA is invested in, but Gabriel did speak with a representative from the large investment company while he was setting up the account. The representative walked him through the steps and recommended a portfolio that would grow, since they were feeling behind in their retirement savings.*

That's tricky advice.

After going over all of this information, I was able to offer Rebecca and Gabriel some advice and some hope. But first, I had to deliver the hard news: you're going to have to work until you're 70. It's not the most appealing idea, but it will put you in a much better situation going forward.

As for your savings, I suggested a few Yellow Money investment tools, ways we could grow their money faster than we could in a Green Money tool, like a CD or annuity. Because they had a small amount of money to start with, money they might need in an emergency, we needed to keep that money liquid while it was growing. I showed them a few ways they could trim their budget and contribute more to their savings over the next few years, growing that retirement account faster.

We decided on a Dividend Stock Portfolio. Even working until 70, Gabriel and Rebecca would need an 8 percent return to be ready to retire in 10 years. As it turned out, we were able to average 18 to 23 percent on their portfolio in the first two years. By year three, they were in such good shape that they only needed 6 percent growth for the next seven years to meet their retirement goals. Rebecca and Gabriel are thrilled and still happily running their church, looking forward to relaxing and becoming part of the retired members of their congregation one day soon.

Like Gabriel and Rebecca, you might own a few retirement accounts or policies, but at the same time have no good sense of your *overall investment strategy*. Do you have one in place? Do you want one that will help you meet your retirement goals? Yellow Money looks at *ALL* your accounts and all their different strategies to create a plan that helps them all work together. Your current investment situation may not reflect your wishes. As a matter of fact, it likely doesn't.

You may have a better understanding of your assets than Janet did, but even someone with an investment strategy can benefit from having a financial professional review their portfolio:

» *Adam is 69 years old. He retired four years ago. He relied on income from an IRA for three years in order to increase his Social Security benefit. He also made significant investments in 36 different mutual funds. He chose to diversify among the funds by selecting a portion for growth, another for good dividends, another that focused on promising small cap companies and a final portion that work like index funds. All the money that Adam had in mutual funds he considered Need Later Money that he wanted to rely on in his 80s. After the stock market took a hit in 2008, Adam lost some confidence in his investments and decided to sit down with a financial professional to see if his portfolio was able to recover.*

The professional Adam met with was able to determine what goals he had in mind. Specifically, the financial professional determined what Adam actually wanted and needed the money for, and when he needed it. His professional also looked inside each of the mutual funds and discovered several instances of overlap. While Adam had created diversity in his portfolio by selecting funds focused on different goals, he didn't account for overlap in the companies in which the funds were invested. Out of the 36 funds, his professional found that 20 owned nearly identical stock. While most of the companies were good investments, the high instance of overlap did not contribute to the healthy investment diversity that Adam wanted. Adam's financial professional also provided him with a report that explained the concentration ratio of his holdings (noting how much of his portfolio was contained within the top 25 stock holdings), the percentage of his portfolio that each company in which he invested in represented (showing the percentage of net assets that each company made up as an overall position in his portfolio) and the portfolio date of his account (showing when the funds in his portfolio were last updated: as funds are required to report updates only twice per year, it was possible that some of his fund reports could be six months old).

Adam's professional consolidated his assets into one investment management strategy. This allowed Charles' investments to be managed by someone he trusted who knew his specific investment goals and needs. Eliminating redundancy and overlap in his portfolio was easy to do but difficult to detect since Adam had multiple funds with multiple brokerage firms. Adam sat down with a professional to see if his mutual funds could perform well, and he left with a consolidated management plan and a money manager that understood him personally. That's Yellow Money at its best.

AVOIDING EMOTIONAL INVESTING

There's no way around it; people get emotional about their money. And for good reason. You've spent your life working for it, exchanging your time and talent for it, and making decisions about how to invest it, save it and make it grow. The maintenance of your lifestyle and your plans for retirement all depend on it. The best investment strategies, however, don't rely on emotions. One of Yellow Money's greatest strengths lies in the fact that it is managed by someone who understands your needs and desires, but doesn't make decisions about your money under the influence of emotion.

A well-managed investment account meets your goals as a whole, not in individualized and piecemeal ways. Professional money managers do this by creating requirements for each type of investment in which they put your money. We'll call them "screens." Your money manager will run your holdings through the screens they have created to evaluate different types of investment strategies. A professionally managed account will only have holdings that meet the requirements laid out in the overall management plan that was designed to meet your investment goals. The holdings that don't make it through the screens, the ones that don't contribute to your investment goals, are sold and redistributed to investments that your financial professional has determined to be appropriate.

Different screens apply to different Yellow Money strategies. For example, if one of your goals is significant growth, which would require taking on more risk alongside the potential for more return, an investment professional would screen for companies that have high rates of revenue and sales growth, high earnings growth, rising profit margins, and innovative products. On the other hand, if you want your portfolio to be used for income, which would call for lower risk and less return, your professional would screen for dividend yield and sector diversification. *Every investor has a different goal, and every goal requires a customized strategy that uses quantitative screens.* A professional will create a portfolio that reflects your investment desires. If some of the current assets you own complement the strategies that your professional recommends, those will likely stay in your portfolio.

Screening your assets removes emotions from the equation. It removes attachment to underperforming or overly risky investments. Financial professionals aren't married to particular stocks or mutual funds for any reason. They go by the numbers and see your portfolio through a lens shaped by your retirement goals. Your professional understands your wants and needs, and creates an investment strategy that takes your life events and future plans into account. It's a planful approach, and it allows you to tap into the tools and resources of a professional who has built a career around successful investing. Managing money is a full-time job and is best left to a professional money manager.

Removing emotions from investing also allows you to be unaffected by the day-to-day volatility of the market. Your financial professional doesn't ask where the market is going to be in a year, three years or a month from now. If you look at the value of the stock market from the beginning of the twentieth century to today, it's going up. Despite the Great Depression, despite the 1987 crash, despite the 2008 market downturn, the market, as a whole, trends up. Remember the major market downturn in 2008 when the market lost 30 percent of its value? Not only did it completely recover, it has far exceeded its 2008 value. Emotional investing led countless people to sell low as the market went down, and buy the same shares back when the market started to recover. That's an expensive way to do business. While you can't afford to lose money that you need in two, three or five years, your Need Later Money has time to grow. The best way to do so is to make it Yellow.

CREATING AN INVESTMENT STRATEGY

Just like Janet and Charles, chances are that you can benefit from taking a more managed investment approach tailored to your goals. Yellow Money is generally Need Later Money that you want to grow for needs you'll have in at least 10 years. You can work with your financial planner to create investments that meet your needs within different timeframes. You may need to rely on some of your Yellow Money in 10, 15 or 20 years, whether for additional income, a large purchase you plan on making or a vacation. Whatever you want it for, you will need it down the road. A financial professional can help you rescale the risk of your assets as they grow, helping you lock in your profits and secure a source of income you can depend on later.

So what does a Yellow Money account look like? Here's what it *doesn't* look like: a portfolio with 49 small cap mutual funds, a dozen individual stocks and an assortment of bond accounts. A brokerage account with a hodgepodge of investments, even if goal-oriented, is not a professionally managed account. It's still Red Money. Remember, Yellow Money is a managed account that has an overarching investment philosophy. When you look at making investments that will perform to meet your future income needs, the burning question becomes: How much should you have in the market and how should it be invested? Working with a professional will help you determine how much risk you should take, how to balance your assets so they will meet your goals and how to plan for the big ticket items, like health care expenses, that may be in your future. Yes, Yellow Money is exposed to risk, but by working with a professional, you can manage that risk in a productive way.

WHY YELLOW MONEY?

If you have met your immediate income needs for retirement, why bother with professionally managing your other assets? The money you have accumulated above and beyond your income needs probably has a greater purpose. It may be for your children or grandchildren. You may want to give money to a charity or organization that you admire. In short, you may want to craft your legacy. It would be advantageous to grow your assets in the best manner possible. A financial professional has built a career around managing money in profitable ways. They are experts under the supervision of the organization that they represent.

Turning to Yellow Money also means that you don't have to burden yourself with the time commitment, the stress, and the cost of determining how to manage your money. Yellow Money can help you better enjoy your retirement. Do you want to sit down in your home office every day and determine how to best allocate your assets, or do you want to be living your life while someone else manages your money for you? When the majority of your Red Money is managed with a specific purpose by a financial professional, you don't have to be worrying about which stocks to buy and sell today or tomorrow.

YELLOW MONEY OPTIONS

Many options exist that provide yellow money investment tools that can grow your money. Just a few examples:

Exchange Traded Funds (ETFs) are investment companies that offer funds, which trade on the market like stocks. ETFs are based on varying investment philosophies. One example is the

Endowment Series by Gradient Investments LLC, which allows individual investors to enjoy the benefits typically only available to large endowment organization. Large university endowment funds enjoy higher-than-average returns because they are able to invest huge amounts of money at once. These larger investments enable them to leverage asset classes that the average individual cannot access. These classes include private equity, absolute return hedge funds, commodities and real estate, classes that have served these organizations very well over time.

Gradient makes it possible for individual investors to use this endowment strategy through ETFs, investing a portion of your portfolio in asset classes that are similar in philosophy to those of the Super Endowment Funds. Because of the unique setup of these asset classes, this Endowment Series ETF
- Delivers superior long-term, risk-adjusted returns
- Offers greater diversification than traditional asset classes
- Opens up investments typically not available to individual investors
- Enables scaled risk exposures depending on personal investment goals

Dividend Stock Portfolios are essentially just what they sound like: portfolios made of stocks that pay dividends. They offer investors steady income and exposure to blue chip (nationally known with reliable returns) stocks. The Gradient 50 "G50" is one kind of dividend stock portfolio, which uses a three-step investment process that selects 50 high-quality, dividend paying stocks. First, they identify financially strong companies that pay reliable, generous dividends. These companies have a long history of profitability, generate consistent cash flow and exceed analyst expectations for earnings. With a balance of steady dividend payers and growth added by the generous dividend payers, G50 portfolios deliver an income stream that can outpace inflation. Diversification is a key part of the dividend stock portfolio, as well. The G50, for example, is created by an investment team that selects only stocks that are diversified across multiple industries. This strategic portfolio construction allows the portfolio to contain the top dividend stocks while also eliminating individual security and individual concentration risks.

Laddered Income Strategies are a method of creating cash flow with fixed income investments. These investments include certificates of deposits (CDs), bond- related exchange traded funds (ETFs), U.S. Treasury notes and individual bonds, agency securities, corporate bonds, and zero coupon bonds. Essentially, the "ladder" is made up of fixed income investments that are diversified by when they mature and mature at regular intervals. When one matures, the manager either reinvests the proceeds at the end of the ladder or puts the money into an account for the owner's expenses.

The Ladder Income Strategy offers a solution for investors who will need their money in the next five years. The ladder preserves your principal while also generating yield, as an equal amount of the portfolio yields each year for a set number of consecutive years (often within a range of three to seven years). Not all ladder strategies are created the same. Many invest in bonds—which are difficult to diversify and can present liquidity problems—or bond mutual funds—which take care of the need for diversification but offer no maturity date. Some ladder strategies, such as Gradient's, invest in diversified, liquid investments that ALSO have defined maturity dates. These sorts of strategies can deliver consistent returns, earn strong average yields, lower your investment risk, provide liquidity and lower expenses.

SEEKING FINANCIAL ADVICE: STOCK BROKERS VS. INVESTMENT ADVISORS

Investors basically have access to two types of advice in today's financial world: advice from stock brokers and advice given by investment advisors. Most investors, however, don't know the difference between types of advice and the people from whom they receive advice. Today, there are two primary types of advice offered to investors: advice given by a commission-based registered representative (brokers) and advice given by fee-based Investment Advisors. Unfortunately, many investors are not aware that a difference exists; nor have they been explained the distinction between the two types of advice. In a survey taken by TD Ameritrade, the top reasons investors choose to work with an independent registered investment advisor are:*

- Registered Investment Advisors are required, as fiduciaries, to offer advice that is in the best interest of clients
- More personalized service and competitive fee structure offered at a Registered Investment Advisor firm
- Dissatisfaction with full commission brokers

The truth is that there is a great deal of difference between stock brokers and investment advisor representatives. For starters, investment advisor representatives are obligated to act in an investor's best interests in every aspect of a financial relationship. Confusion continues to exist among investors struggling to find the best financial advice out there and the most credible sources of advice.

Here is some information to help clear up the confusion so you can find good advice from a professional you can trust:

- Investment advisors have the fiduciary duty to act in a client's best interest at all times with every investment decision they make. Stock brokers and brokerage firms usually do not act as fiduciaries to their investors and are not obligated to make decisions that are entirely in the best interest of their customers. For example, if you decide you

---

*2011 Advisor Sentiment Study, commissioned by TD AMERITRADE. TD Ameritrade, Inc.

want to invest in precious metals, a stock broker would offer you a precious metals account from their firm. An Investment Advisor would find you a precious metals account that is the best fit for you based on the investment strategy of your portfolio.
- Investment advisors give their clients a Form ADV describing the methods that the professional uses to do business. An Investment Advisor also obtains client consent regarding any conflicts of interest that could exist with the business of the professional.
- Stock brokers and brokerage firms are not obligated to provide comparable types of disclosure to their customers.
- Whereas stock brokers and firms routinely earn large profits by trading as principal with customers, Investment Advisors cannot trade with clients as principal (except in very limited and specific circumstances).
- Investment Advisors charge a pre-negotiated fee with their clients in advance of any transactions. They cannot earn additional profits or commissions from their customers' investments without prior consent. Registered Investment Advisors are commonly paid an asset-based fee that aligns their interests with those of their clients. Brokerage firms and stock brokers, on the other hand, have much different payment agreements. Their revenues may increase regardless of the performance of their customers' assets.
- Unlike brokerage firms, where investment banking and underwriting are commonplace, Registered Investment Advisors must manage money in the best interests of their customers. Because Registered Investment Advisors charge set fees for their services, their focus is on their client. Brokerage firms may focus on other aspects of the firm that do not contribute to the improvement of their clients' assets.

- Unlike brokers, Registered Investment Advisors do not get commissions from fund or insurance companies for selling their investment products.

Just to drive home the point, here is what a fiduciary duty to a client means for a Registered Investment Advisor. Registered Investment Advisors must:*

- Always act in the best interest of their client and make investment decisions that reflect their goals.
- Identify and monitor securities that are illiquid.
- When appropriate, employ fair market valuation procedures.
- Observe procedures regarding the allocation of investment opportunities, including new issues and the aggregation of orders.
- Have policies regarding affiliated broker-dealers and maintenance of brokerage accounts.
- Disclose all conflicts of interest.
- Have policies on use of brokerage commissions for research.
- Have policies regarding directed brokerage, including step-out trades and payment for order flow.
- Abide by a code of ethics.

---

*2011 Advisor Sentiment Study, commissioned by TD AMERITRADE. TD Ameritrade, Inc.

CHAPTER 8 RECAP //

- Yellow Money may make Red Money less dangerous.
- Yellow Money is professionally managed.
- Yellow Money has a cohesive purpose and a strategy behind it.
- If you haven't sat down and thought about how much money you need in order to generate income during retirement, you're just speculating.
- Red Money is like driving yourself in unfamiliar territory. With Yellow Money, you are still traveling by car, but now you have a professional driving on your behalf.
- The deck is stacked against the ordinary investor. According to the DALBAR report, individual investors consistently underperform compared to the market because of a variety of factors, including emotional investing.
- Yellow Money is managed without emotions.
- Yellow Money investment options, such as ETFs, dividend stock portfolios and ladder income strategies, offer methods for investing your money in a lower-risk, managed way that can outpace inflation and grow your money for future needs.
- Checking your truly Red Money should be like checking the sports section. You are interested in it, but it won't directly affect your lifestyle. If your Red Money goes down 50 percent, no one should have to scrape you off the floor.

9
THE BALANCED FORMULA FOR INVESTING

In Chapter 1, we discussed how today's investment options require advice that is relevant to today. Traditional, outdated investment strategies are not only ineffective, they can be harmful to the average investor. One of the most traditional ways of thinking about investing is the risk versus reward trade-off. It goes something like this.

Investment options that are considered safer carry less risk, but also offer the potential for less return. Riskier investment options carry the burden of volatility and a greater potential for loss, but they also offer a greater potential for large rewards. Most professionals move their clients back and forth along this range, shifting between investments that are safer and investments that are structured for growth. Essentially, the old rules of investing dictate that you can either choose relative safety *or* return, but you can't have both.

Updated investment strategies work with the flexibility of liquidity to remake the rules. Here is how:

There are three dimensions that are inherent in any investment: *Liquidity, Safety,* and *Return*. You can maximize any two of these dimensions at the expense of the third. If you choose Safety and Liquidity, this is like keeping your assets in a checking account or savings account. This option delivers a lot of Safety and Liquidity, but at the expense of any Return. On the other hand, if you choose Liquidity and Return, meaning you have the potential for great return and can still reclaim your money whenever you choose, you will likely be exposed to a very high level of risk.

Understanding Liquidity can help you break the old Risk versus Safety trade-off. By identifying assets from which you don't require Liquidity, you can place yourself in a position to potentially profit from relatively safe investments that provide a higher than average rate of return.

Choosing Safety and Return over Liquidity can have significant impacts on the accumulation of your assets. In Oskar's case, the paradigm shift from earning and saving to leveraging assets was a costly one.

> » *Oskar has been farming corn and hay on his 1,200 acres of land for forty years. He learned to farm from his Icelandic father, who also taught him his mistrust of the market. As a result, Oskar keeps most of his money in an FDIC insured bank, with somewhere between $40,000 and $80,000 in his checking and savings accounts, depending on the time of year. He has a good reason: if your combine fails during the harvest, you have to be able to repair or replace it if you don't want to lose your crop.*
>
> *But when Oskar retires, even though he no longer needs large amounts of cash on hand, he makes no changes. His accounts continue to be full to the brim, earning little to no*

interest and doing nothing to further secure his retirement. Oskar feels ok about this because at least, he thinks, his money is safe. Then, when he sells the farm, he puts even more money into these accounts. Those accounts, unfortunately, don't even earn enough money to keep pace with inflation. Oskar believes that all investment agents give advice that makes the agent money, not Oskar, and so he never gets a professional opinion. Sadly, this means Oskar's money is losing value every day. He was a successful farmer, and he could be well positioned for a safe, happy retirement.

Now, what Oskar really needs is some good advice. Fortunately, Oskar has a granddaughter, and she's determined to help him get that advice. She takes him to the financial professional who helps her parents. Just for her Oskar decides to listen.

As you can see, choosing Liquidity solely can be a costly option. The sooner you want your money back, the less you can leverage it for Safety or Return. If you have the option of putting your money in a long-term investment, you will be sacrificing Liquidity, but potentially gaining both Safety and Return. Rethinking your approach to money in this way can make a world of difference and can provide you with a structured way to generate income while allowing the value of your asset to grow over time.

The question is, how much Liquidity do you **really** need? Think about it. If you haven't sat down and created an income plan for your retirement, your perceived need for Liquidity is a guess. You don't know how much cash you'll need to fill the income gap if you don't know the amount of your Social Security benefit of the total of your other income options. If you *have* determined your income need and have made a plan for filling your income gap, you can partition your assets based on when you will need them.

With an income plan in place, *you can use new rules to enjoy both Safety and Return from your assets.*

CHAPTER 9 RECAP //
- Investment Advisors are obligated to make investment decisions or recommendations that are in your best interests and are aligned with your financial situation, time frame and risk tolerance, and to put your interests ahead of their own. Stock brokers and brokerage firms are obligated to make suitable recommendations from the universe of products they are permitted to sell.

10
TAX STRATEGY FOR RETIREMENT SUCCESS

Most of us accept taxes the way we accept that there will be rainy days. It's just the way things are. Every now and then, taxes must be paid. But what if you could choose when your rainy days happen? What if you accepted that you were going to have to have a handful of rainy days, but you could employ a strategy that shortened those rain showers or made sure they never fell on a picnic or a trip to the park?

In retirement, a good tax strategy won't prevent you from having to pay taxes, but it *can* ensure that you aren't paying too much or at the wrong time. It's all about using the right form.

How can a tax form do all that? The answer lies in planning. **Tax planning** and **tax reporting** are two very different things. Most people only *report* their taxes. March rolls around, people pull out their 1040s or use TurboTax to enter their income and taxable assets, and ship it off to Uncle Sam at the IRS. If you use a CPA to report your taxes, you are essentially paying them to record history. You have the option of being proactive with your taxes and to plan for your future by making smart, informed decisions about how taxes affect your overall financial plan. Working with a financial professional who, along with a CPA, makes recommendations about your finances to you, will keep you looking forward instead of in the rearview mirror as you enter retirement.

TAXES AND RETIREMENT

When you retire, you move from the earning and accumulation phase of your life into the asset distribution phase of your life. For most people, that means relying on Social Security, a 401(k), an IRA, or a pension. Wherever you have put your Green or Yellow Money for retirement, you are going to start relying on it to provide you with the income that once came as a paycheck. Most of these distributions will be considered income by the IRS and will be taxed as such. There are exceptions to that (not all of your Social Security income is taxed, and income from Roth IRAs is not taxed), but for the most part, your distributions will be subject to income taxes.

Regarding assets that you have in an IRA or a 401(k) plan that uses an IRA, when you reach 70 ½ years of age, you will be required to draw a certain amount of money from your IRA as income each year. That amount depends on your age and the balance in your IRA. The amount that you are required to withdraw as income is called a Required Minimum Distribution (RMD). Why are you required to withdraw money from your own account? Chances are the money in that account has grown over time, and the government wants to collect taxes on that growth. If you have a large balance in an IRA, there's a chance your RMD could increase your income significantly enough to put you into a higher tax bracket, subjecting you to a higher tax rate.

Here's where tax planning can really begin to work strongly in your favor. In the distribution phase of your life, you have a predictable income based on your RMDs, your Social Security benefit and any other income-generating assets you may have. What really impacts you at this stage is how much of that money you keep in your pocket after taxes. Essentially, **you will make more money saving on taxes than you will by making more money.** If you can reduce your tax burden by 30, 20 or even 10 percent, you earn yourself that much more money by not paying it in taxes.

How do you save money on taxes? By having a plan. In this instance, a financial professional can work with the CPAs at their firm to create a distribution plan that minimizes your taxes and maximizes your annual net income.

BUILDING A TAX DIVERSIFIED PORTFOLIO

So far so good: avoid taxes, maximize your net annual income and have a plan for doing it. When people decide to leverage the experience and resources of a financial professional, they may not be thinking of how distribution planning and tax planning will benefit their portfolios. Often more exciting prospects like planning income annuities, investing in the market and structuring investments for growth rule the day. Taxes, however, play a crucial role in retirement planning. Achieving those tax goals requires knowledge of options, foresight and professional guidance.

Finding the path to a good tax plan isn't always a simple task. Every tax return you file is different from the one before it because things constantly change. Your expenses change. Planned or unplanned purchases occur. Health care costs, medical bills, an inheritance, property purchases, reaching an age where your RMD kicks in or travel, any number of things can affect how much income you report and how many deductions you take each year.

Preparing for the ever-changing landscape of your financial life requires a tax-diversified portfolio that can be leveraged to balance the incomes, expenditures and deductions that affect you each year. A financial professional will work with you to answer questions like these:
- What does your tax landscape look like?
- Do you have a tax-diversified portfolio robust enough to adapt to your needs?
- Do you have a diversity of taxable and non-taxable income planned for your retirement?
- Will you be able to maximize your distributions to take advantage of your deductions when you retire?
- Is your portfolio strong enough and tax-diversified enough to adapt to an ever-changing (and usually increasing) tax code?

» May was really ready to get out of the hospital. She hadn't really wanted this hip replacement, but her daughters, sister and brothers all insisted. You don't want to be in wheelchair, they reminded her. And they were right. May loves to garden. So she had the hip replacement, and she wore a huge grin as they wheeled her out of the hospital and to her daughter's car. On the way home, she called her sister and brothers to report happily that she's was finally heading home. One call she didn't think to make: her CPA.

May's operation, hospital stay, medication and the continuing physical therapy she will require come to a total of more than $50,000.

Currently, Americans can deduct medical expenses that are more than 7.5 percent of their Adjusted Gross Income (AGI). May's AGI is $60,000 the year of her knee replacement, meaning she is able to deduct $44,000 of her medical bills from her taxes that year. Her AGI dictated that she could *deduct more than 80 percent of her medical expenses that year.* ***But May didn't know this.***

Had she been working with a financial professional who regularly asked her about any changes in her life, her spending, or her expenses (expected or unexpected), May could have saved thousands of dollars. May can also file an amendment to her tax return to recoup the overpayment.

This relatively simple example of how tax planning can save you money is just the tip of the iceberg. No one can be expected to know the entire U.S. tax code. But a professional who is working with a team of CPAs and financial professionals have an advantage over the average taxpayer who must start from square one on their own every year. Have you been taking advantage of all the deductions that are available to you?

PROACTIVE TAX PLANNING

The implications of proactive tax planning are far reaching, and are larger than many people realize. Remember, doing your taxes in January, February, March or April means you are writing a history book. Planning your taxes in October, November or December means that you are writing the story as it happens. You can look at all the factors that are at play and make decisions that will impact your tax return *before* you file it.

Realizing that tax planning is an aspect of financial planning is an important leap to make. When you incorporate tax planning into your financial planning strategy, it becomes part of the way you maximize your financial potential. Paying less in taxes means you keep more of your money. Simply put, the more money you keep, the more of it you can leverage as an asset. This kind of planning can affect you at any stage of your life. If you are 40 years old, are you contributing the maximum amount to your 401(k) plan? Are you contributing to a Roth IRA? Are you finding ways to structure the savings you are dedicating to your children's education? Do you have life insurance? Taxes and tax planning affects all of these investment tools. Having a relationship with a professional who works with a CPA can help you build a truly comprehensive financial plan that not only works with your investments, but also shapes your assets to find the most efficient ways to prepare for tax time. There may be years that you could benefit from higher distributions because of the tax bracket that you are in, or there could be years you would benefit from taking less. There may be years when you have a lot of deductions and years you have relatively few. Adapting your distributions to work in concert with your available deductions is at the heart of smart tax planning. Professional guidance can bring you to the next level of income distribution, allowing you to remain flexible enough to maximize your tax efficiency. And remember, saving money on taxes makes you more money than making money does.

What you have on paper is important: your assets, savings, investments, which are financial expression of your work and time. It's just as important to know how to get it off the paper in a way that keeps most of it in your pocket. Almost anything that involves financial planning also involves taxes. Annuities, investments, IRAs, 401(k)s, 403(b), and many other investment options will have tax implications. Life also has a way of throwing curveballs. Illness, expensive car repair or replacement, or ***any event that has a financial impact on your life will likely have a corresponding tax implication*** around which you should adapt your financial plan. Tax planning does just that.

One dollar can end up being less than 25 cents to your heirs.

> » *Nash and his father, Ben, were close. That's why, when Ben passed away, Nash knew that not only was he the beneficiary of Ben's $500,000 IRA, but also that Ben had intended for*

much of that IRA to fund Nash's four children's college educations.

Nash is 50 when his father's estate is distributed. Nash is focused on honoring his father's wishes, and his oldest twin sons are entering college. Nash immediately liquidates his father's IRA to pay their tuition. Unfortunately, this well-intentioned decision puts Nash into a 39.6 tax bracket for the year. After taxes, Ben's IRA was reduced to $302,000. Nash also has to pay an additional 3.8 percent surtax on the net investment income, bringing the inheritance down to $283,000. Nash's regular income isn't immune either: after all of this, his regular income will be subject to a 43.4 percent tax rate for the year.

Then come the state taxes, an additional 9 percent, and estate taxes on top of all that claim another 22 percent. When all is said and taxed, the IRS has levied a 75 percent tax on Ben's legacy, leaving Nash's family a total of $125,000, rather than $500,000. It's money they're grateful for, but it's far less than Ben had hoped to give to his grandkids.

As the above example makes clear, leaving an asset to your beneficiaries can be more complicated than it may seem. In the case of a traditional IRA, after federal, estate and state taxes, the asset could literally diminish to as little as 25 percent of its value.

How does working with a professional help you make smarter tax decisions with your own finances? Any financial professional worth their salt will be working with a firm that has a team of trained tax professionals, including CPAs, who have an intimate knowledge of the tax code and how to adapt a financial plan to it.

Here's another example of how taxes have major implications on asset management:

» *Esteban and Betty, a 62-year-old couple, begin working with a financial professional in October. After structuring their assets to reflect their risk tolerance and creating assets that would provide them Green Money income during retirement, they feel good about their situation. They make decisions that allow them to maximize their Social Security benefits, they have plenty of options for filling their income gap, and have begun a safe yet ambitious Yellow Money strategy with their professional. When their professional asks them about their tax plan, they tell him their CPA handled their taxes every year, and did a great job. Their professional says, "I don't mean who does your taxes, I mean, who does your tax planning?" Esteban and Betty aren't sure how to respond.*

Their professional brings Esteban and Betty's financial plan to the firm's CPA and has her run a tax projection for them. A week later their professional calls them with a tax plan for the year that will save them more than $3,000 on their tax return. The couple is shocked. A simple piece of advice from the CPA based on the numbers revealed that if they paid their estimated taxes before the end of the year, they would be able to itemize it as a deduction, allowing them to save thousands of dollars.

This solution won't work for everyone, and it may not work for Esteban and Betty every year. That's not the point. By being proactive with their approach to taxes and using the resources made available by their financial professional, they were able to create a tax plan that saved them money.

YELLOW MONEY AND TAXES

There are also tax implications for the money that you have managed professionally. People with portions of their investment portfolio that are actively traded can particularly benefit from having a proactive tax strategy. Without going into too much detail, for tax purposes there are two kinds of investment money: qualified and non-qualified. Different investment strategies can have different effects on how you are taxed on your investments and the growth of your investments. Some are more beneficial for one kind of investment strategy over another. Determining how to plan for the taxation of non-qualified and qualified investments is fodder for holiday party discussions at accounting firms. While it may not be a stimulating topic for the average investor, you don't have to understand exactly how it works in order to benefit from it.

While there are many differences between qualified and non-qualified investments, the main difference is this: qualified plans are designed to give investors tax benefits by deferring taxation of their growth until they are withdrawn. Non-qualified investments are not eligible for these deferral benefits. As such, non-qualified investments are taxed whenever income is realized from them in the form of growth.

Actively and non-actively traded investments provide a simple example of how to position your investments for the best tax advantage. In an actively traded and managed portfolio, there is a high amount of buying and selling of stocks, bonds, funds, ETFs, etc. If that active portfolio of non-qualified investments does well and makes a 20 percent return one year and you are in the 39.6 percent tax bracket, your net gain from that portfolio is only about 12 percent (39.6 percent tax of the 20 percent gain is roughly 8 percent.) In a passive trading strategy, you can use a qualified investment tool, such as an IRA, to achieve 13, 14 or 15 percent growth (much lower than the actively traded portfolio), but still realize a higher net return because the growth of the qualified investment is not taxed until it is withdrawn.

Does this mean that you have to always rely on a buy and hold strategy in qualified investment tools? Not necessarily. The question is, if you have qualified and non-qualified investments, where do you want to position your actively traded and managed assets? Incorporating a planful approach to positioning your investments for more beneficial taxation can be done many ways, but let's consider one example. Keeping your actively managed investment strategies inside an IRA or some other qualified plan could allow you to realize the higher gains of those investments without paying tax on their growth every year. Your more passively managed funds could then be kept in taxable, non-qualified vehicles and methods, and because you aren't realizing income from them on an annual basis by frequently trading them, they grow sheltered from taxation.

If you are interested in taking advantage of tax strategies that maximize your net income, you need the attentive strategies, experience and knowledge of a professional who can give you options that position you for profit. At the end of the day, what's important to you as the consumer is how much you keep, your after-tax take home.

ESTATE TAXES

The government doesn't just tax your income from investments while you're alive. They will also dip into your legacy.

While estate taxes aren't as hot of a topic as they were a few years ago, they are still an issue of concern for many people with assets. While taxes may not apply on estates that are less than $5 million, certain states have estate taxes with much lower exclusion ratios. Some are as low as $600,000. Many people may have to pay a state estate tax. One strategy for avoiding those types of taxes is to move assets outside of your estate. That can include gifting them to family or friends, or putting them into an irrevocable trust. Life insurance is another option for protecting your legacy.

11
PREDICTING THE FUTURE OF TAXES

Unfortunately, there's no tax-predicting crystal ball. But we can look at tax levels today (historically low) and tax trends over the course of American history and we can make an educated guess: taxes go up. Sadly, we hear this same threat so often that it has begun to sound like the boy who cried wolf. The reason behind this lies in the fact that tax hikes usually do not take effect until two or three years after their introduction and subsequently get piecemeal implementation. The result of this prolonged implementation period can be equated to death by a thousand paper cuts.

DEBT CEILING – CAUSE AND EFFECTS
The raising of the debt ceiling raised more than just the ability for our government to go further into debt. It also raised concerns and fears about the future of our economy. We are now

seeing major swings in the markets with investors showing serious concerns over the future of investment valuations and their personal wealth. Unfortunately, the reasoning behind all of this uncertainty is preceded by the inability to see the full implications of what is in store. We rarely talk about the fact that the discussions on raising the debt ceiling were coupled to discussions on major tax reforms needed to correct the problems underlining the debt ceiling increase itself.

Increasing the debt ceiling was needed because the government maxed out its credit card, so to speak, which it has been living off of for quite some time. It is really not much different than what we have been seeing from the general public for the past few decades. Unfortunately, most of us do not have the ability to get a credit limit increase on our credit cards once we reach the maximum limit unless we can show the ability to pay this balance back. The only way to pay this credit card back is by spending less and making more money.

This is exactly where the federal government is today. They have been given a higher credit limit, but they still must find a way to decrease the spending while making more money. The only way the government makes money is by collecting taxes.

Unfortunately, at the current moment, the government is collecting approximately $120 billion less per month than it currently spends. Discussions for major tax reform have accompanied the discussions for the increased debt ceiling.

DEBT AND EARNINGS

Let us take a closer look at where we are today. The U.S. national debt is increasing at an alarming rate, rising to levels never seen before and threatening serious harm to the economy. Through the end of 2010, the national debt has risen to $13.6 trillion, averaging an 11.4 percent increase annually over the past five years and a 9.2 percent increase annually over the past 10 years. To put this into perspective, the national gross domestic product (GDP) has increased to $14.5 trillion during the same period, averaging a 2.9 percent annual increase over the past five years and a 3.9 percent increase over the past 10 years. At the end of 2010, the national debt level was 93 percent of the GDP. Economists believe that a sustainable economy exists at a maximum level of approximately 80 percent. As of December 20,2013, the U.S. national debt is 107.69 percent of GDP with the debt at $17.252 trillion and the GDP at $16.020 trillion.* The significance of these two numbers lies within the contrast. The national debt is the amount that needs to be repaid. This is the credit card balance. Gross domestic product on the other hand is less known and represents the market value of all final goods and services produced within a country during a given period. Essentially, GDP represents the gross taxable income available to the government. If debts are increasing at a greater rate than the gross income available for taxation, then the only way to make up the difference is by increasing the rate at which the gross income is taxed.

The most recent presidential budget shows a continuing trend in the disparity between growth in the national debt and GDP over the next two decades. Although the increasing disparity is a real concern and shows that, at least in the short run, the federal deficit will not be addressed to counteract the potential crisis ahead, it is the revenue collection that tells the disconcerting story. Over the past 40 years the average collection of GDP has been approximately 17.6 percent and currently collections are at approximately 14.4 percent of GDP.

As the presidential budget reveals, the projected revenues are estimated to be 20 percent by the end of the next decade. That is a 38.8 percent increase from the current tax levels. To put this into perspective, if you are currently in the top tax bracket of

---

*http://www.usdebtclock.org/ 12/20/13

35 percent and this bracket increases by the proposed collection increase, your tax rate will be approximately 48.5 percent. Keep in mind that even at this rate the deficit is projected to increase.

2013 – THE END OF AN ERA?
From a historical point of view, taxes are extremely low. The last time the U.S. national debt was at the same percentage level of GDP as today was at the end of World War II and several years following. The maximum tax rate averaged 90 percent from 1944 through 1963. Compare that to the maximum rate of 39.6 percent today and it becomes very clear that there is a disparity of extreme proportions.

Taxes during this historical period were at extreme levels for nearly 20 years, during and following this current level of debt-to-GDP. A significant point to note about the difference between that time and today is the economic activity. The period of 1944 through 1963 was in the heart of both the industrial revolution and the birth of the Baby Boom generation. Today, we are mired in extreme volatility with frequent periods of boom and bust at the same time we are witnessing the beginning of the greatest retirement wave ever experienced within the U.S. economy.

To contrast these two time periods with respect to the recovery period is irrelevant as the external pressures from globalization and domestic unfunded liabilities did not exist or were irrelevant factors during the prior period.

To add insult to injury, U.S. domestic unfunded liabilities are currently estimated somewhere around $61.6 trillion due to items such as Social Security, Medicare and government pensions. The most concerning part of this pertains to the coming wave of retirement as the Baby Boom generation begins retiring and drawing on the unfunded Social Security for which they currently have entitlement. Over the long run, expenditures related to healthcare programs such as Medicare and Medicaid are projected to grow faster than the economy overall as the population matures.

To put unfunded liabilities into perspective, consider these as off-balance-sheet obligations similar to those of Enron. Although these are not listed as part of the national debt, they must be paid. These liabilities exist outside of the annual budgetary debt discussed. The difference between Enron and the U.S. unfunded liabilities is that if the U.S. government cannot come up with the funds to pay all these liabilities through revenue generation, they will print the money necessary to pay the debt.

WHAT DOES THE SOLUTION LOOK LIKE?

Unfortunately, the general public is in a no-win situation for this solution to the problem. Printing money does not bode well for economic growth. This creates inflationary pressures that devalue the U.S. dollar and make everyone less wealthy. Cutting the entitlements that compose this liability leaves millions of people without benefits they have come to expect. The only other option, and one that the government knows all too well, is increasing taxes. In fact, according to a Congressional Budget Office paper issued in 2004:

"The term 'unfunded liability' has been used to refer to a gap between the government's projected financial commitment under a particular program and the revenues that are expected to be available to fund that commitment. But no government obligation can be truly considered 'unfunded' because of the U.S. government's sovereign power to tax – which is the ultimate resource to meet its obligations."

A balanced budget will be required at some point and with this will come higher taxes. We have uncertainty surrounding tax rates and how high they will go. At that time, extensions put in place in December 2010 on Bush-era tax cuts are set to expire. We are likely to see some tax increases at this point. Whether it is only on the top earners or unilaterally across all income levels is yet to be seen, but an increase of some sort will most certainly occur.

How do you prepare? Why spend so much time reassuring you that taxes will increase? Because you have an opportunity to take action. Now is the time to prepare for what will come and structure countermeasures for the good, the bad and the ugly of each of these legislative nightmares through tax-advantaged retirement planning.

You make more money by saving on taxes than you do by making more money. The simplistic logic of the statement makes sense when you discover it takes $1.50 in earnings to put that same dollar, saved in taxes, back in your pocket.

As simple as it sounds, it is much more difficult to execute. Most people fail to put together a plan as they near retirement, beginning with a simple cash flow budget. If you have not analyzed your proposed income streams and expenses, you could not possibly have taken the time to position these cash flows and other events into a tax-preferred plan.

Most people will state that they have a plan and, thus, do not need any further assistance in this area. The truth in most instances is that people could not show you their plan, and among the few that could, most would not be able to show you how they have executed it. In this regard, they might as well be Richard Nixon stating, "I am not a crook" for as much as they state, "I have a plan." The truth lies in waiting. As we approach or begin retirement, we should look at what cash flows we will have. Do we have a pension? How about Social Security? How much additional cash flow am I going to need to draw from my assets to maintain the lifestyle that I desire?

We spend our whole lives saving and accumulating wealth but spend so little time determining how to distribute this accumulation so as to retain it. We need to make sure we have the appropriate diversification of taxable versus non-taxable assets to complement our distribution strategy.

THE BENEFITS OF DIVERSIFICATION

Heading into retirement, we should be situated with a diversified tax landscape. The point to spending our whole lives accumulating wealth is not to see the size of the number on paper, but rather to be an exercise in how much we put in our pocket after removing it from the paper. To truly understand tax diversification, we must understand what types of money exist and how each of these will be treated during accumulation and, most importantly, during distribution. The following is a brief summary:
1. Free money
2. Tax-advantaged money
3. Tax-deferred money
4. Taxable money
    a. Ordinary income
    b. Capital gains and qualified dividends

FREE MONEY

Free money is the best kind of money regardless of tax treatment because, in the end, you have more money than you would have otherwise. Many employers will provide contributions toward employee retirement accounts to offer additional employment benefits and encourage employees to save for their own retirement. With this, employers often will offer a matching contribution in which they contribute up to a certain percentage of an employee's salary (generally three to five percent) toward that employee's retirement account when the employee contributes to their retirement account as well. For example, if an employee earns $50,000 annually and contributes three percent ($1,500) to their retirement account annually, the employer will also contribute three percent ($1,500) to the employee's account. That is

$1,500 in free money. Take all you can get! Bear in mind that any employer contribution to a 401(k) will still be subject to taxation when withdrawn.

TAX-ADVANTAGED MONEY

Tax-advantaged money is the next best thing to free money. Although you have to earn tax-advantaged money, you do not have to give part of it away to Uncle Sam. Tax-advantaged money comes in three basic forms that you can utilize during your lifetime; four if prison inspires your future, but we are not going to discuss that option.

One of the most commonly known forms of tax-advantaged money is municipal bonds, which earn and pay interest that could be tax-advantaged on the federal level, or state level, or both. There are several caveats that should be discussed with regard to the notion of tax-advantaged income from municipal bonds. First, you will notice that tax-advantaged has several flavors from the state and federal perspective. This is because states will generally tax the interest earned on a municipal bond unless the bond is offered from an entity located within that state. This severely limits the availability of completely tax-advantaged municipal bonds and constrains underlying risk and liquidity factors. Second, municipal bond interest is added back into the equation for determining your modified adjusted gross income (MAGI) for Social Security. This could push your income above a threshold and subject a portion of your Social Security income to taxation.

In effect, if this interest subjects some other income to taxation then this interest is truly being taxed.

Last, municipal bond interest may be excluded from the regular federal tax system, but it is included for determining tax under the alternative minimum tax (AMT) system. In its basic form, the AMT system is a separate tax system that applies if the tax computed under AMT exceeds the tax computed under the regular tax system. The difference between these two computations is the alternative minimum tax.

TAX-ADVANTAGED MONEY: ROTH IRA

Roth accounts are probably the single greatest tax asset that has come from Congress outside of life insurance. They are well known but rarely used. Roth IRAs were first established by the Taxpayer Relief Act of 1997 and named after Senator William Roth, the chief sponsor of the legislation. Roth accounts are simply an account in the form of an individual retirement account or an employer sponsored retirement account that allows for tax-advantaged growth of earnings and, thus, tax-advantaged income.

The main difference between a Roth and a traditional IRA or employer-sponsored plan lies in the timing of the taxation. We are all very familiar with the typical scenario of putting money away for retirement through an employer plan, whereby they deduct money from our paychecks and put it directly into a retirement account. This money is taken out before taxes are calculated, meaning we do not pay tax on those earnings today. A Roth account, on the other hand, takes the money after the taxes have been removed and puts it into the retirement account, so we do pay tax on the money today. The other significant difference between these two is taxation during distribution in later years. Regarding our traditional retirement accounts, when we take the money out later it is added to our ordinary income and is taxed accordingly. Additionally, including this in our income subjects us to the consequences mentioned above for municipal bonds with Social Security taxation, AMT, as well as higher Medicare premiums. A Roth on the other hand is distributed tax-advantaged and does not contribute toward negative impact items such as Social Security taxation, AMT, or Medicare premium increases. It essentially comes back to us without tax and other obligations.

The best way to view the difference between the two accounts is to look at the life of a farmer. A farmer will buy seed, plant it in the ground, grow the crops and harvest it later for sale. Typically, the farmer would only pay tax on the crops that have been harvested and sold. But if you were the farmer, would you rather pay tax on the $5,000 of seed that you plant today or the $50,000 of crops harvested later? The obvious answer is $5,000 of seed today. The truth to the matter is that you are a farmer, except you plant dollars into your retirement account instead of seeds into the earth.

So why doesn't everyone have a Roth retirement account if things are so simple? There are several reasons, but the single greatest reason has been the constraints on contributions. If you earned over certain thresholds (MAGI over $125,000 single and $183,000 joint for 2012), you were not eligible to make contributions, and until last year, if your modified adjusted gross income (MAGI) was over $100,000 (single or joint), you could not convert a traditional IRA to a Roth. Outside these contribution limits, most people save for retirement through their employers and most employers do not offer Roth options in their plans. The reason behind this is because Roth accounts are not that well understood and people have been educated to believe that saving on taxes today is the best possible course of action.

TAX-ADVANTAGED MONEY: LIFE INSURANCE

As previously mentioned, the single greatest tax asset that has come from Congress outside of life insurance is the Roth account. Life insurance is the little-known or little-discussed tax asset that holds some of the greatest value in your financial history both during life and upon death. It is by far the best tax-advantaged device available. We traditionally view life insurance as a way to protect our loved ones from financial ruin upon our demise and it should be noted that everyone who cares about someone should have life insurance. Purchasing a life insurance policy ensures that our loved ones will receive income from the life insurance company to help them pay our final expenses and carry on with their lives without us comfortably when we die. The best part of the last gift you leave is the fact that nobody will have to pay tax on the money received. This is the single greatest tax-advantaged device available, but it has one downside, we do not get to use it. Only our heirs will.

There are new permanent life insurance options that help cover the cost of long term care. A qualifying event could be a cognitive impairment such as Alzheimer's or Parkinson's disease, or generally if two of six activities of daily living (ADL's) are met. ADL's include the inability to do any of the following:
- Bathing
- Dressing
- Eating
- Functional Mobility
- Personal Hygiene
- Toilet Hygiene

If a policyholder cannot meet two of these six ADL's, then the insurance company will payout a portion of the death benefit each month (typically two percent of the death benefit) to cover qualified long term care costs including home health care, assisted living care, and nursing home care costs. This is a living benefit that is income tax free to the policyholder. For an individual who does not wish to purchase traditional long term care insurance, this is a good alternative. One way or another, a tax free benefit is paid out!

Permanent life insurance policies also have cash value benefits built in that allows the policyholder, while still living, the ability to pull the cash value portion of the plan with favorable tax consequences. Using the loan feature of the plan, a person can reduce or eliminate any tax consequences of a withdrawal. The government taxes life insurance cash value withdrawals using last in, first out (LIFO) taxation. The principal amount that is invested into the plan is considered by the government to be the amount withdrawn first from the policy. The gains are taxed only when the principal payments of the life insurance plan have been withdrawn. That is another unique tax advantage of life insurance. Due to the mortality and administrative charges that exist within permanent life insurance plans, it usually takes a minimum of 10 years for an investor to have enough cash value built up in the account to exceed their principal contributions. For this reason, I rarely recommend life insurance as a growth or investment vehicle.

Refer to chapter 14 for a more complete discussion on life insurance.

TAX-DEFERRED MONEY

Tax-deferred money is the type of money with which most people are familiar, but we also briefly reviewed the idea above. Tax-deferred money is typically our traditional IRA, employer sponsored retirement plan or a non-qualified annuity. Essentially, you put money into an investment vehicle that will accumulate in value over time and you do not pay taxes on the earnings that grow these accounts until you distribute them. Once the money is distributed, taxes must be paid. However, the same negative consequences exist with regard to additional taxation and expense in other areas as previously discussed. The cash accumulation value can be used for tax-advantaged income.

TAXABLE MONEY

Taxable money is everything else and is taxable today, later or whenever it is received. These four types of money come down to two distinct classifications: taxable and tax-free. The greatest difference when comparing taxable and tax-advantaged income is a function of how much money we keep after tax. For help in determining what the differences should be, excluding outside factors such as Social Security taxation and AMT, a tax equivalent yield should be used.

TAX-ADVANTAGED IN THE REAL WORLD

To put the tax equivalent yield into perspective, let us look at an example: Bob and Mary are currently retired, living on Social Security and interest from investments and falling within the 25 percent tax bracket. They have a substantial portion of their investments in municipal bonds yielding 6 percent, which is quite comforting in today's market. The tax equivalent yield they would need to earn from a taxable investment would be 8 percent, a 2 percent gap that seems almost impossible given current market volatility. However, something that has never been put into perspective is that the interest from their municipal bonds is subject to taxation on their Social Security benefits (at 21.25 percent). With this, the yield on their municipal bonds would be 4.725 percent, and the taxable equivalent yield falls to 6.3 percent, leaving a gap of only 1.575 percent.

In the end, most people spend their lives accumulating wealth through the best, if not the only vehicle they know, a tax-deferred account. This account is most likely a 401(k) or 403(b) plan offered through our employer and may be supplemented with an IRA that was established at one point or another. As the years go by, people blindly throw money into these accounts in an effort to save for a retirement that we someday hope to reach.

The truth is, most people have an age selected for when they would like to retire, but spend their lives wondering if they will ever be able to actually quit working. To answer this question, you must understand how much money you will have available to contribute toward your needs. ***In other words, you need to know what your after-tax income will be during this period.***

All else being equal, it would not matter if you put your money into a taxable, tax-deferred or tax-advantaged account as long as income tax rates never change and outside factors are never an event. The net amount you receive in the end will be the same.

Unfortunately, this will never be the case. We already know that taxes will increase in the future, meaning we will likely see higher taxes in retirement than during our peak earning years.

Regardless, saving for retirement in any form is a good thing as it appears from all practical perspectives that future government benefits will be cut and taxes will increase. You have the ability to plan today for efficient tax diversification and maximization of our after-tax dollars during your distribution years.

12
FINDING THE FREE BRIDGE

Louis Brandeis provides one of the best examples illustrating how tax planning works. Brandeis was Associate Justice on the Supreme Court of the United States from 1916 to 1939. Born in Louisville, Kentucky, Brandeis was an intelligent man with a touch of country charm. He described tax planning this way:

"I live in Alexandria, Virginia. Near the Court Chambers, there is a toll bridge across the Potomac. When in a rush, I pay the dollar toll and get home early. However, I usually drive outside the downtown section of the city and cross the Potomac on a free bridge.

The bridge was placed outside the downtown Washington, D.C. area to serve a useful social service – getting drivers to drive the extra mile and help alleviate congestion during the rush hour.

If I went over the toll bridge and through the barrier without paying a toll, I would be committing tax evasion.

> *If I drive the extra mile and drive outside the city of Washington to the free bridge, I am using a legitimate, logical and suitable method of tax avoidance, and I am performing a useful social service by doing so.*
>
> *The tragedy is that **few people know that the free bridge exists.***"

Like Brandeis, most American taxpayers have options when it comes to "crossing the Potomac," so to speak. It's a financial planner's job to tell you what options are available. You can wait until March to file your taxes, at which time you might pay someone to report and pay the government a larger portion of your income. However, you could instead file before the end of the year, work with your financial professional and incorporate a tax plan as part of your overall financial planning strategy. Filing later is like crossing the toll bridge. Tax planning is like crossing the free bridge.

Which would you rather do?

The answer to this question is easy. Most people want to save money and pay less in taxes. What makes this situation really difficult in real life, however, is that the signs along the side of the road that direct us to the free bridge are not that clear. To normal Americans, and to plenty of people who have studied it, the U.S. tax code is easy to get lost in. There are all kinds of rules, exceptions to rules, caveats and conditions that are difficult to understand, or even to know about. What you really need to know is your options and the bottom line impacts of those options.

ROTH IRA CONVERSIONS

The attractive qualities of Roth IRAs may have prompted you to explore the possibility of moving some of your assets into a Roth account. Another important difference between the accounts is how they treat Required Minimum Distributions (RMDs). When you turn 70 ½ years old, you are required to take a minimum amount of money out of a traditional IRA. This amount is your

FINDING THE FREE BRIDGE

RMD. It is treated as taxable income. Roth IRAs, however, do not have RMDs, and their distributions are not taxable. Quite a deal, right?

While having a Roth IRA as part of your portfolio is a good idea, converting assets to a Roth IRA can pose some challenges, depending on what kinds of assets you want to transfer.

One common option is the conversion of a traditional IRA to a Roth IRA. You may have heard about converting your IRA to a Roth IRA, but you might not know the full net result on your income. The main difference between the two accounts is that the growth of investments within a traditional IRA is not taxed until income is withdrawn from the account, whereas taxes are charged on contribution amounts to a Roth IRA, not withdrawals. The problem, however, is that when assets are removed from a traditional IRA, even if the assets are being transferred to a Roth IRA account, taxes apply.

There are a lot of reasons to look at Roth conversions. People have a lot of money in IRAs, up to multiple millions of dollars. Even with $500,000, when they turn 70 ½ years old, their RMD is going to be approximately $18,000, and they have to take that out whether they want to or not. It's a tax issue. Essentially, if you will be subject to high RMDs, it could have impacts on how much of your Social Security is taxable, and on your tax bracket.

By paying taxes now instead of later on assets in a Roth IRA, you can realize tax-advantaged growth. You pay once and you're done paying. Your heirs are done paying. It's a powerful tool. Here's a simple example to show you how powerful it can be:

Imagine that you pay to convert a traditional IRA to a Roth. You have decided that you want to put the money in a vehicle that gives you a tax-advantaged income option down the road. If you pay a 25 percent tax on that conversion and the Roth IRA then doubles in value over the next 10 years, you could look at your situation as only having paid 12.5 percent tax.

The prospect of tax-advantaged income is a tempting one. While you have to pay a conversion tax to transfer your assets, you also have turned taxable income into tax free retirement money that you can let grow as long as you want without being required to withdraw it.

There are options, however, that address this problem. Much like the Brandeis story, there may be a "free bridge" option for many investors.

Here are some of the things to consider before converting to a Roth IRA:

- If you make a conversion before you retire, you may end up paying higher taxes on the conversion because it is likely that you are in some of your highest earning years, placing you in the highest tax bracket of your life. It is possible that a better strategy would be to wait until after you retire, a time when you may have less taxable income, which would place you in a lower tax bracket.
- Many people opt to reduce their work hours from fulltime to part-time in the years before they retire. If you have pursued this option, your income will likely be lower, in turn lowering your tax rate.
- The first years that you draw Social Security benefits can also be years of lower reported income, making it another good time frame in which to convert to a Roth IRA.

One key strategy to handling a Roth IRA conversion is to *always be able to pay the cost of the tax conversion with outside money*. Structuring your tax year to include something like a significant deduction can help you offset the conversion tax. This way you aren't forced to take the money you need for taxes from the value of the IRA. The reason taxes apply to this maneuver is because when you withdraw money from a traditional IRA, it is treated as taxable income by the IRS. Your financial professional, with the help of the CPAs at their firm, may be able to provide you with options like after-tax money, itemized deductions or other situations that can pose effective tax avoidance options.

Some examples of avoiding Roth IRA conversions taxes include:

- *Using medical expenses that are above 10 percent of your Adjusted Gross Income.* If you have health care costs that you can list as itemized deductions, you can convert an amount of income from a traditional IRA to a Roth IRA that is offset by the deductible amount. Essentially, deductible medical expenses negate the taxes resulting from recording the conversion.
- *Individuals, usually small business owners, who are dealing with a Net Operating Loss (NOL).* If you have NOLs, but aren't able to utilize all of them on your tax return, you can carry them forward to offset the taxable income from the taxes on income you convert to a Roth IRA.
- *Charitable giving.* If you are charitably inclined, you can use the amount of your donations to reduce the amount of taxable income you have during that year. By matching the amount you convert to a Roth IRA to the amount your taxable income was reduced by charitable giving, you can essentially avoid taxation on the conversion. You may decide to double your donations to a charity in one year, giving them two years' worth of donations in order to offset the Roth IRA conversion tax on this year's tax return.
- *Investments that are subject to depletion.* Certain investments can kick off depletion expenses. If you make an investment and are subject to depletion expenses, they can be deducted and used to offset a Roth IRA conversion tax.

Not all of the above scenarios work for everyone, and there are many other options for offsetting conversion taxes. The point is that you have options, and your financial professional and tax professional can help you understand those options.

If you have a traditional IRA, Roth conversions are something you should look at. As you approach retirement you should consider your options and make choices that keep more of your money in your pocket, not the governments.

ADDITIONAL TAX BENEFITS OF ROTH IRAS
Not only do Roth IRAs provide you with tax-advantaged growth, they also give you a tax diversified landscape that allows you to maximize your distributions. Chances are that no matter the circumstances, you will have taxed income and other assets subject to taxation. *But if you have a Roth IRA, you have the unique ability to manage your Adjusted Gross Income (AGI), because you have a tax-advantaged income option!*

Converting to a Roth IRA can also help you preserve and build your legacy. Because Roth IRAs are exempt from RMDs, after you make a conversion from a traditional IRA, your Roth account can grow tax-advantaged for another 15, 20 or 25 years and it can be used as tax-advantaged income by your heirs. It is important to note, however, that non-spousal beneficiaries do have to take RMDs from a Roth IRA, or choose to stretch it and draw tax-advantaged income out of it over their lifetime.

TO CONVERT OR NOT TO CONVERT?
Conversions aren't only for retirees. You can convert at any time. Your choice should be based on your individual circumstances and tax situation. Sticking with a traditional IRA or converting to a Roth, again, depends on your individual circumstances, including your income, your tax bracket and the amount of deductions you have each year.

Is it better to have a Roth IRA or traditional IRA? It depends on your individual circumstance. Some people don't mind having taxable income from an IRA. Their income might not be very high and their RMD might not bump their tax bracket up, so it's not as big a deal. A similar situation might involve income from Social Security. Social Security benefits are taxed based on other income you are drawing. If you are in a position where none or very little of your Social Security benefit is subject to taxes, paying income tax on your RMD may be very easy.

> » *There are also situations where leveraging taxable income from a traditional IRA can work to your advantage come tax time. For example, Johnny and Pat dream of buying a boat when they retire. It is something they have looked forward to their entire marriage. In addition to the savings and investments that they created to supply them with income during retirement, which includes a traditional IRA, they have also saved money for the sole purpose of purchasing a boat once they stop working.*
>
> *When the time comes and they finally buy the boat of their dreams, they pay an additional $15,000 in sales taxes that year because of the large purchase. Because they are retired and earning less money, the deductions they used to be able to realize from their income taxes are no longer there. The high amount of sales taxes they paid on the boat puts them in a position where they could benefit from taking taxable income from a traditional IRA.*
>
> *When Johnny and Pat's financial professional learns about their purchase, he immediately contacts a CPA at his firm to run the numbers. They determine that by taking a $15,000 distribution from their IRA, they could fulfill their income needs to offset the $15,000 sales tax deduction that they were claiming due to the purchase of their boat. In the end, they pay zero taxes on their income distribution from their IRA.*

The moral of the story? ***Having a tax diversified landscape gives you options.*** Having capital assets that can be liquidated, tax-advantaged income options and sources that can create capital gains or capital losses will put you in a position to play your cards right no matter what you want to accomplish with your taxes. The ace up your sleeve is your financial professional and the CPAs they work with. Do yourself a favor and *plan* your taxes instead of *reporting* them!

CHAPTER 12 RECAP //

- You make more money by saving on taxes than you do by making more money. This simple concept becomes extremely valuable to people in retirement and those living on fixed incomes.
- When you report your taxes, you are paying to record history. When you *plan* your taxes with a financial professional, you are proactively finding the best options for your tax return.
- The future of U.S. taxation is uncertain. You know what the tax rate and landscape is today, but you won't tomorrow. The only thing you can really count on is the trend of increasing taxation.
- Look for the "free bridge" option in your tax strategy.
- Converting from a traditional to a Roth IRA can provide you with tax-advantaged retirement income.
- Converting to a Roth IRA can also help you preserve and build your legacy.
- There are many ways to reduce your taxes. Being smart about your Roth IRA conversion is one of the main ways to do so.

13
WHAT DOES LEGACY MEAN TO YOU?

Thinking about what's happening in the world after you're gone isn't always the happiest of activities. For that reason, estate planning is often at the very bottom of a very long list of to-dos—way below things like "get a root canal" and "clean out the gutters." But here's a suggestion: imagine the people you love or the causes that inspire you. Next, envision them in a scenario that would be life-changing for them. Imagine how happy they are, how much easier the future will be.

Now, how can you help them get there?

It's an important task, since you are the person most likely to look out for those people and causes. If you don't plan your legacy, someone else will. That someone else is usually a combination of the IRS and other government entities: lawyers, executors, courts, and accountants. Who do you think has the best interests of your beneficiaries in mind?

Today, there is more consideration given to planning a legacy than just maximizing your estate. When most people think about an estate, it may seem like something only the very wealthy have: a stately manor or an enormous business. But a legacy is something else entirely. A legacy is more than the sum total of the financial assets you have accumulated. It is the lasting impression you make on those you leave behind. The dollar and cents are just a small part of a legacy.

A legacy encompasses the stories that others tell about you, shared experiences and values. An estate may pay for college tuition, but a legacy may inform your grandchildren about the importance of higher education and self-reliance.

A legacy may also contain family heirlooms or items of emotional significance. It may be a piece of art your great-grandmother painted, family photos, or a childhood keepsake.

When you go about planning your legacy, certainly explore strategies that can maximize the financial benefit to the ones you care about. But also take the time to ensure that you have organized the whole of your legacy, and let that be a part of the last gift you leave.

Many people avoid planning their legacy until they feel they must. Something may change in your life, like the birth of a grandchild, the diagnosis of a serious health problem, or the death of a close friend or loved one. Waiting for tragedy to strike in order to get your affairs in order is not the best course of action. The emotional stress of that kind of situation can make it hard to make patient, thoughtful decisions. Taking the time to create a premeditated and thoughtful legacy plan will assure that your assets will be transferred where and when you want them when the time comes.

THE BENEFITS OF PLANNING YOUR LEGACY

The distribution of your assets, whether in the form of property, stocks, Individual Retirement Accounts, 401(k)s or liquid assets, can be a complicated undertaking if you haven't left clear instructions about how you want them handled. Not having a plan will cost more money and take more time, leaving your loved ones to wait (sometimes for years) and receive less of your legacy than if you had a clear plan.

Planning your legacy will help your assets be transferred with little delay and little confusion. Instead of leaving decisions about how to distribute your estate to your family, attorneys or financial professionals, preserve your legacy and your wishes by drafting a clear plan at an early age.

And while you know all that, it can still be hard to sit down and do it. It reminds you that life is short, and the relatively complicated nature of sorting through your assets can feel like a daunting task. But one thing is for sure: ***it is impossible for your assets to be transferred or distributed the way you want at the end of your life if you don't have a plan.***

Ask yourself:
- Are my assets up to date?
- Have my primary and contingent beneficiaries been clearly designated?
- Does my plan allow for restriction of a beneficiary?
- Does my legacy plan address minor children that I want to provide with income?
- Does my legacy plan allow for multi-generational payout?

Answers to these questions are critical if you want the final say in how your assets are distributed. In order to achieve your legacy goals, you need a plan.

MAKING A PLAN

Eventually, when your income need is filled and you have sufficient standby money to meet your need for emergencies, travel or other extra expenses you are planning for, whatever isn't used during your lifetime becomes your financial legacy. The money that you do not use during your lifetime will either go to loved ones, unloved ones, charity, or the IRS. The question is, who would you rather disinherit?

By having a legacy plan that clearly outlines your assets, your beneficiaries and your distribution goals, you can make sure that your money and property is ending up in the hands of the people you determine beforehand. Is it really that big of a deal? It absolutely is. Think about it. Without a clear plan, it is impossible for anyone to know if your beneficiary designations are current and reflect your wishes because you haven't clearly expressed who your beneficiaries are. You may have an idea of who you want your assets to go to, but without a plan, it is anyone's guess. It is also impossible to know if the titling of your assets is accurate unless you have gone through and determined whose name is on the titles. More importantly, *if you have not clearly and effectively communicated your desires regarding the planned distribution of your legacy, you and your family may end up losing a large part of it.*

As you can see, managing a legacy is more complicated than having an attorney read your will, divide your estate and write checks to your heirs. The additional issue of taxes, Family Maximum Benefit calculations and a host of other decisions rear their heads. Educating yourself about the best options for positioning your legacy assets is a challenging undertaking. Working with a financial professional who is versed in determining the most efficient and effective ways of preserving and distributing your legacy can save you time, money and strife.

So, how do you begin?

Making a Legacy Plan Starts with a Simple List. The first, and one of the largest, steps to setting up an estate plan with a financial professional that reflects your desires is creating a detailed inventory of your assets and debts (if you have any). You need to know what assets you have, who the beneficiaries are, how much they are worth and how they are titled. You can start by identifying and listing your assets. This is a good starting point for working with a financial professional who can then help you determine the detailed information about your assets that will dictate how they are distributed upon your death.

If you are particularly concerned about leaving your kids and grandkids a lifetime of income with minimal taxes, you will want to discuss a Stretch IRA option with your financial professional.

STRETCH IRAS: GETTING THE MOST OUT OF YOUR MONEY

In 1986, the U.S. Congress passed a law that allows for multi-generational distributions of IRA assets. This type of distribution is called a Stretch IRA because it stretches the distribution of the account out over a longer period of time to several beneficiaries. It also allows the account to continue accumulating value throughout your relatives' lifetimes. You can use a Stretch IRA as an income tool that distributes throughout your lifetime, your children's lifetimes and your grandchildren's lifetimes.

Stretch IRAs are an attractive option for those more concerned with creating income for their loved ones than leaving them with a lump sum that may be subject to a high tax rate. With traditional IRA distributions, non-spousal beneficiaries must generally take distributions from their inherited IRAs, whether transferred or not, within five years after the death of the IRA owner. An exception to this rule applies if the beneficiary elects to take distributions over his or her lifetime, which is referred to as stretching the IRA.

Beneficiaries Stretch IRA Distributions

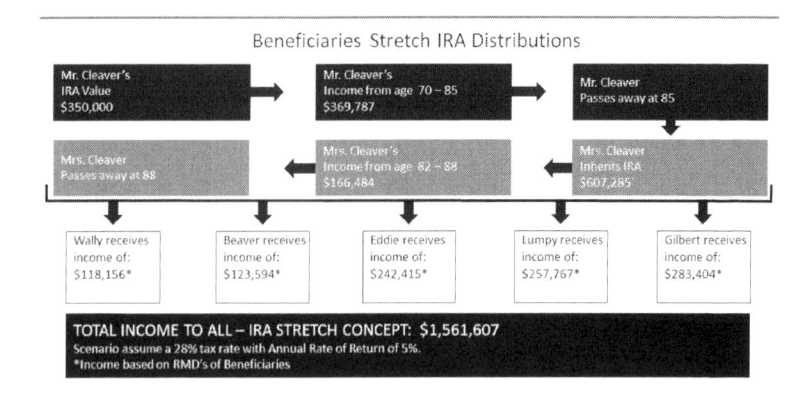

Mr. Cleaver's IRA Value $350,000	Mr. Cleaver's Income from age 70 – 85 $369,787	Mr. Cleaver Passes away at 85
Mrs. Cleaver Passes away at 88	Mrs. Cleaver's Income from age 82 – 88 $166,484	Mrs. Cleaver Inherits IRA $607,285

| Wally receives income of: $118,156* | Beaver receives income of: $123,594* | Eddie receives income of: $242,415* | Lumpy receives income of: $257,767* | Gilbert receives income of: $283,404* |

TOTAL INCOME TO ALL – IRA STRETCH CONCEPT: $1,561,607
Scenario assume a 28% tax rate with Annual Rate of Return of 5%.
*Income based on RMD's of Beneficiaries

Beneficiaries FAIL to Stretch IRA Distributions

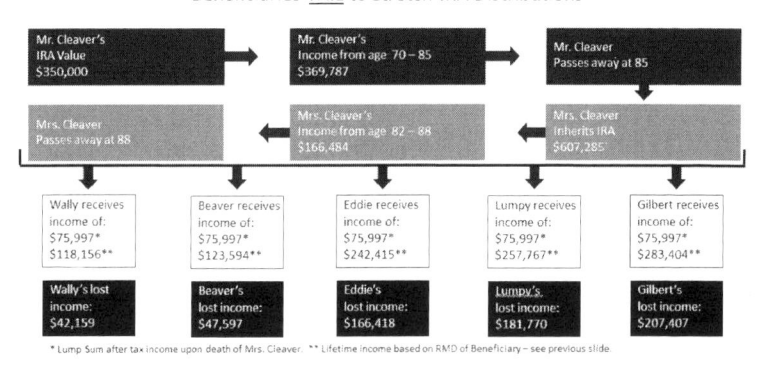

Mr. Cleaver's IRA Value $350,000	Mr. Cleaver's Income from age 70 – 85 $369,787	Mr. Cleaver Passes away at 85
Mrs. Cleaver Passes away at 88	Mrs. Cleaver's Income from age 82 – 88 $166,484	Mrs. Cleaver Inherits IRA $607,285

| Wally receives income of: $75,997* $118,156** | Beaver receives income of: $75,997* $123,594** | Eddie receives income of: $75,997* $242,415** | Lumpy receives income of: $75,997* $257,767** | Gilbert receives income of: $75,997* $283,404** |
| Wally's lost income: $42,159 | Beaver's lost income: $47,597 | Eddie's lost income: $166,418 | Lumpy's lost income: $181,770 | Gilbert's lost income: $207,407 |

* Lump Sum after tax income upon death of Mrs. Cleaver.   ** Lifetime Income based on RMD of Beneficiary – see previous slide.

Let's begin by looking at the potential of stretching an IRA across multiple generations.

> » *In this scenario, Mr. Quinn has an IRA with a current balance of $350,000. If we assume a five percent annual rate of return, and a 28 percent tax rate, the Stretch IRA turned a $502,625 legacy into more than $1.5 million. Doubling the value of the IRA also provided Mr. Quinn, his wife, two children and three grandchildren with income. Not choosing*

the stretch option would have cost nearly $800,000 and had impacts on six of Mr. Quinn's loved ones.

Unfortunately, many things may also play a role in failing to stretch IRA distributions. It can be tempting for a beneficiary to take a lump sum of money despite the tax consequences. Fortunately, if you want to solidify your plan for distribution, there are options that will allow you to open up an IRA and incorporate "spendthrift" clauses for your beneficiaries. This will ensure your legacy is stretched appropriately and to your specifications. Only certain insurance companies allow this option, and you will not find this benefit with any brokerage accounts. You need to work with a financial professional who has the appropriate relationship with an insurance company that provides this option.

14
MAKING YOUR MARK: YOUR LEGACY

» *Glenn organized his assets long ago. He started planning his retirement early and made investment decisions that would meet his needs. With a combination of IRA to Roth IRA conversions, a series of income annuities and a well-planned money management strategy overseen by his financial professional, he easily filled his income gap and was able to focus on ways to accumulate his wealth throughout his retirement. He reorganized his Know So and Hope So Money as he got older. When Glenn retired, he had an income plan created that allowed him to maximize his Social Security benefit. He even had enough to accumulate wealth during his retirement. At this point, Glenn turned his attention to planning his legacy. He wanted to know how he could maximize the amount of his legacy he will pass on to his heirs.*

> *Glenn met with an attorney to draw up a will, but he quickly learned that while having a will was a good plan, it wasn't the most efficient way to distribute his legacy. In fact, relying solely on a will created several roadblocks.*

The two main problems that arose for Glenn were *Probate* and *Unintentional Disinheritance:*

PROBLEM #1: PROBATE
Probate. Just speaking the word out loud can cause shivers to run down your spine. Probate's ugly reputation is well deserved. It can be a costly, time consuming process that diminishes your estate and can delay the distribution of your estate to your loved ones. Nasty stuff, by any measure. Unless you have made a clear legacy plan and discussed options for avoiding probate, it is highly likely that you have many assets that might pass through probate needlessly. ***If your will and beneficiary designations aren't correctly structured, some of these assets will go through the probate process, which can turn dollars into cents.***

If you have a will, probate is usually just a formality. There is little risk that your will won't be executed per your instructions. The problem arises when the costs and lengthy timeline that probate creates come into play. Probate proceedings are notoriously expensive, lengthy and ponderous. A typical probate process identifies all of your assets and debts, pays any taxes and fees that you owe (including estate tax), pays court fees, and distributes your property and assets to your heirs. This process can take months or even years. For this reason, and because of the sometimes exorbitant fees that may be charged by lawyers and accountants during the process, probate has earned a nasty reputation.

Probate can also be a painstakingly public process. Because the probate process happens in court, the assets you own that go through a probate procedure become part of the public record.

While this may not seem like a big deal to some, other people don't want that kind of intimate information available to the public.

Additionally, if your estate is entirely distributed via your will, the money that your family may need to cover the costs of your medical bills, funeral expenses and estate taxes will be tied up in probate, which can last up to a year or more. While immediate family members may have the option of requesting immediate cash from your assets during probate to cover immediate health care expenses, taxes, and fees, that process comes with its own set of complications. Choosing alternative methods for distributing your legacy can make life easier for your loved ones and can help them claim more of your estate in a more timely fashion than traditional methods.

A simpler and less tedious approach is to avoid probate altogether by structuring your estate to be distributed outside of the probate process. Two common ways of doing this are by structuring your assets inside a life insurance plan, and by using individual retirement planning tools like IRAs that give you the option of designating a beneficiary upon your death.

PROBLEM #2: UNINTENTIONALLY DISINHERITING YOUR FAMILY

You would never want to unintentionally disinherit a loved one or loved ones because of confusion surrounding your legacy plan. Unfortunately, it happens. Why? This terrible situation is typically caused by a simple lack of understanding. In particular, mistakes regarding legacy distribution occur with regards to those whom people care for the most: their grandchildren.

One of the most important ways to plan for the inheritance of your grandchildren is by properly structuring the distribution of your legacy. Specifically, you need to know if your legacy is going to be distributed *per stirpes* or *per capita*.

Per Stirpes. *Per stirpes* is a legal term in Latin that means "by the branch." Your estate will be distributed *per stirpes* if you designate each branch of your family to receive an equal share of your estate. In the event that your children predecease you, their share will be distributed evenly between their children — your grandchildren.

Per Capita. *Per capita* distribution is different in that you may designate different amounts of your estate to be distributed to members of the same generation.

Per stirpes distribution of assets will follow the family tree down the line as the predecessor beneficiaries pass away. On the other hand, per capita distribution of assets ends on the branch of the family tree with the death of a designated beneficiary. For example, when your child passes away, in a per capita distribution, your grandchildren would not receive distributions from the assets that you designated to your child.

What the terms mean is not nearly as important as what they do, however. The reality is that improperly titled assets could accidentally leave your grandchildren disinherited upon the death of their parents. It's easy to check, and it's even easier to fix.

A simple way to remember the difference between the two types of distribution goes something like this: "***Stripes are forever and Capita is capped.***"

Another way to avoid complicated legacy distribution problems, and the probate process, is by leveraging a life insurance plan.

LIFE INSURANCE: AN IMPORTANT LEGACY TOOL

One of the most powerful legacy tools you can leverage is a good life insurance policy. Life insurance is a highly efficient legacy tool because it creates money when it is needed or desired the most. Over the years, life insurance has become less expensive, while it offers more features, and it provides longer guarantees.

There are many unique benefits of life insurance that can help your beneficiaries get the most out of your legacy. Some of them include:
- Providing beneficiaries with a tax-free, liquid asset.
- Covering the costs associated with your death.
- Providing income for your dependents.
- Offering an investment opportunity for your beneficiaries.
- Covering expenses such as tuition or mortgage down payments for your children or grandchildren.

Very few people want life insurance, but nearly everyone wants what it does. Life insurance is specifically, and uniquely, capable of creating money when it is needed most. When a loved one passes, no amount of money can remove the pain of loss. And certainly, money doesn't solve the challenges that might arise with losing someone important.

It has been said that when you have money, you have options. When you don't have money, your options are severely limited. You might imagine a life insurance policy can give your family and loved ones options that would otherwise be impossible.

> *» Kelvin spent the last 20 years building a small business. In so many ways, it is a family business. Each of his three children, Heidi, Josephine and Michael, worked in the shop part-time during high school. But after all three attended college, only Heidi returned to join her father, and eventually will run the business full-time when Kelvin retires.*
>
> *Kelvin is able to retire comfortably on Social Security and on-going income from the shop, but the business is nearly his entire financial legacy. It is his wish that Heidi own the business outright, but he also wants to leave an equal legacy to each of his three children.*

> *There is no simple way to divide the business into thirds and still leave the business intact for Heidi.*
>
> *Kelvin ends up buying a life insurance policy to make up the difference. Josephine and Michael will receive their share of an inheritance in cash from the life insurance policy and Heidi will be able to inherit the business intact.*
>
> *Kelvin is able to accomplish his goals, treat all three children equitably and leave Heidi the business she helped to build.*

If you have a life insurance policy but you haven't looked at it in a while, you may not know how it operates, how much it is worth and how it will be distributed to your beneficiaries. You may also need to update your beneficiaries on your policy. In short, without a comprehensive review of your policy, you don't really know where the money will go or to whom it will go.

If you don't have a life insurance policy but are looking for options to maintain and grow your legacy, speaking with a professional can show you the benefits of life insurance. Many people don't consider buying a life insurance policy until some event in their life triggers it, like the loss of a loved one, an accident or a health condition.

BENEFITS OF LIFE INSURANCE

Life insurance is a useful and secure tool for contingency planning, ensuring that your dependents receive the assets that you want them to have, and for meeting the financial goals you have set for the future. While it bears the name "Life Insurance," it is, in reality, a diverse financial tool that can meet many needs. The main function of a life insurance policy is to provide financial assets for your survivors. Life insurance is particularly efficient at achieving this goal because it provides a tax-advantaged lump sum of money in the form of a death benefit to your beneficiary or beneficiaries. That financial asset can be used in a number of ways. It can be structured as an investment to provide income for your spouse or children, it can pay down debts, and it can be used to cover estate taxes and other costs associated with death.

Tax liabilities on the estate you leave behind are inevitable. Capital property, for instance, is taxed at its fair market value at the time of your death, unless that property is transferred to your spouse. If the property has appreciated during the time you owned it, taxation on capital gains will occur. Registered Retirement Savings Plans (RRSPs) and other similarly structured assets are also included as taxable income unless transferred to a beneficiary as well. Those are just a few examples of how an estate can become subject to a heavy tax burden. The unique benefits of a life insurance policy provide ways to handle this tax burden, solving any liquidity problems that may arise if your family members want to hold onto an illiquid asset, such as a piece of property or an investment. Life insurance can provide a significant amount of money to a family member or other beneficiary, and that money is likely to remain exempt from taxation or seizure.

One of life insurance's most important benefits is that it is not considered part of the estate of the policy holder. The death benefit that is paid by the insurance company goes exclusively to the beneficiaries listed on the policy. This shields the proceeds of the policy from fees and costs that can reduce an estate, including probate proceedings, attorneys' fees and claims made by creditors. The distribution of your life insurance policy is also unaffected by delays of the estate's distribution, like probate. Your beneficiaries will get the proceeds of the policy in a timely fashion, regardless of how long it takes for the rest of your estate to be settled.

Investing a portion of your assets in a life insurance policy can also protect that portion of your estate from creditors. If you owe money to someone or some entity at the time of your death, a creditor is not able to claim any money from a life insurance policy or an annuity, for that matter. An exception to this rule is if you had already used the life insurance policy as collateral against a loan. If a large portion of the money you want to dedicate to your legacy is sitting in a savings account, investment or other liquid form, creditors may be able to receive their claim on it before your beneficiaries get anything; that is if there's anything left. A life insurance policy protects your assets from creditors and ensures that your beneficiaries get the money that you intend them to have.

HOW MUCH LIFE INSURANCE DO YOU NEED?

Determining the type of policy and the amount right for you depends on an analysis of your needs. A financial professional can help you complete a needs analysis that will highlight the amount of insurance that you require to meet your goals. This type of personalized review will allow you to determine ways to continue providing income for your spouse or any dependents you may have. A financial professional can also help you calculate the amount of income that your policy should replace to meet the needs of your beneficiaries and the duration of the distribution of that income.

You may also want to use your life insurance policy to meet any expenses associated with your death. These can include funeral costs, fees from probate and legal proceedings, and taxes. You may also want to dedicate a portion of your policy proceeds to help fund tuition or other expenses for your children or grandchildren. You can buy a policy and hope it covers all of those costs, or you can work with a professional who can calculate exactly how much insurance you need and how to structure it to meet your goals. Which would you rather do?

AVOIDING POTENTIAL SNAGS

There are benefits to having life insurance supersede the direction given in a will or other estate plan, but there are also some potential snags that you should address to meet your wishes. For example, if your will instructs that your assets be divided equally between your two children but your life insurance beneficiary is listed as just one of the children, the assets in the life insurance policy will only be distributed to the child listed as the beneficiary. The beneficiary designation of your life insurance supersedes your will's instruction. This is important to understand when designating beneficiaries on a policy you purchase. Work with a professional to make sure that your beneficiaries are accurately listed on your assets, especially your life insurance policies.

USING LIFE INSURANCE TO BUILD YOUR LEGACY

Depending on your goals, there are strategies you can use that could multiply how much you leave behind. Life insurance is one of the most surefire and efficient investment tools for building a substantial legacy that will meet your financial goals.

Here is a brief overview of how life insurance can boost your legacy:

- Life insurance provides an immediate increase in your legacy.
- It provides an income tax-advantaged death benefit for your beneficiaries.
- A good life insurance policy has the opportunity to accumulate value over time.
- It may have an option to include long-term care (LTC) or chronic illness benefits should you require them.

If your income needs for retirement are met and you have Green or Yellow Money assets that will provide for your future expenses, you may have extra assets that you want to earmark as legacy funds.

By electing to invest those assets into a life insurance policy, you can immediately increase the amount of your legacy. Remember, life insurance allows you to transfer a tax-advantaged lump sum of money to your beneficiaries. It remains in your control during your lifetime, can provide for your long-term care needs and bypasses probate costs. And make no mistake, taxes can have a huge impact on your legacy. Not only that, income and assets from your legacy can have tax implications for your beneficiaries, as well.

Here's a brief overview of how taxes could affect your legacy and your beneficiaries:
- The higher your income, the higher the rate at which it is taxed.
- Withdrawals from qualified plans are taxed as income.
- What's more, when you leave a large qualified plan, it ends up being taxed at a high rate.
- If you left a $500,000 IRA to your child, they could end up owing as much as $140,000 in income taxes.
- However, if you could just withdraw $50,000 a year, the tax bill might only be $10,000 per year.

How could you use that annual amount to leave a larger legacy? Luckily, you can leverage a life insurance policy to avoid those tax penalties, preserving a larger amount of your legacy and freeing your beneficiaries from an added tax burden.

> » *When Loretta turned 70 years old, she decided it was time to look into life insurance policy options. She still feels young, but she remembers that her mother died in her early 70s, and she wants to plan ahead so she can pass on some of her legacy to her grandchildren just like her grandmother did for her.*
>
> *Loretta doesn't really want to think about life insurance, but she does want the security, reliability and tax-advantaged*

distribution that it offers. She lives modestly, and her Social Security benefit meets most of her income needs. As the beneficiary of her late husband's Certificate of Deposit (CD), she has $100,000 in an account that she has never used and doesn't anticipate ever needing since her income needs were already met.

*After looking at several different investment options with an professional, Loretta decides that a Single Premium life insurance policy fits her needs best. She can buy the policy with a $100,000 one-time payment and she is guaranteed that it would provide more than the value of the contract to her beneficiaries. If she left the money in the CD, it would be subject to taxes. But for every dollar that she puts into the life insurance policy, her beneficiaries are guaranteed at least that dollar plus a death benefit, and all of it will be **tax-free!***

For $100,000, Loretta's particular policy offers a $170,000 death benefit distribution to her beneficiaries. By moving the $100,000 from a CD to a life insurance policy, Loretta increases her legacy by 70 percent. Not only that, she has also sheltered it from taxes, so her beneficiaries will be able to receive $1.70 for every $1.00 that she entered into the policy! While buying the policy doesn't allow her to use the money for herself, it does allow her family to benefit from her well-planned legacy.

MAKE YOUR WISHES KNOWN

Estate taxes used to be a much hotter topic in the mid-2000s when the estate tax limits and exclusions were much smaller and taxed at a higher rate than today. In 2008, estates valued at $2 million or more were taxed at 45 percent. Just two years later, the limit was raised to $5 million dollars taxed at 35 percent. The limit has continued to rise ever since. The limit applies to fewer people than before. Estate organization, however, is just as important as ever, and it affects everyone.

Ask yourself:
- Are your assets actually titled and held the way you think they are?
- Are your beneficiaries set up the way you think they should be?
- Have there been changes to your family or those you desire as beneficiaries?

There is more to your legacy beyond your property, money, investments and other assets that you leave to family members, loved ones and charities. Everyone has a legacy beyond money. You also leave behind personal items of importance, your values and beliefs, your personal and family history, and your wishes. Beyond a will and a plan for your assets, it is important that you make your wishes known to someone for the rest of your personal legacy. When it comes time for your family and loved ones to make decisions after you are gone, knowing your wishes can help them make decisions that honor you and your legacy, and give meaning to what you leave behind. Your professional can help you organize.

Think about your:
- Personal stories / recollections
- Values
- Personal items of emotional significance
- Financial assets
- Do you want to make a plan to pass these things on to your family?

WORKING WITH A PROFESSIONAL

Part of using life insurance to your greatest advantage is selecting the policy and provider that can best meet your goals. Venturing into the jungle of policies, brokers and salespeople can be overwhelming, and can leave you wondering if you've made the best decision. Working with a trusted financial professional can help you cut through the red tape, the "sales-speak" and confusion to find a policy that meets your goals and best serves your desires for your money. If you already have a policy, a financial professional can help you review it and become familiar with the policy's premium, the guarantees the policy affords, its performance, and its features and benefits. A financial professional can also help you make any necessary changes to the policy.

> *» When Patsy turned 88, her daughter finally convinced her to meet with a financial professional to help her organize her assets and get her legacy in order. Although Patsy is reluctant to let a stranger in on her personal finances, she ends up very glad that she did.*
>
> *In the process of listing Patsy's assets and her beneficiaries, her professional finds a man's name listed as the beneficiary of an old annuity that she owns. It turns out, the man is Patsy's ex-husband who is still alive. Had Patsy passed away before her ex-husband, the annuities and any death benefits that came with them, would have been passed on to her ex-husband. This does not reflect her latest wishes.*

Things change, relationships evolve and the way you would like your legacy organized needs to adapt to the changes that happen throughout your life. There may be a new child or grandchild in your family, or you may have been divorced or remarried. A professional will regularly review your legacy assets and ask you questions to make sure that everything is up to date and that the current organization reflects your current wishes.

CHAPTER 14 RECAP //

- You can structure your assets in ways that maximize distributions to your beneficiaries.
- Working with a financial professional can help ensure that many of your assets avoid the ponderous and expensive probate process.
- A financial professional can help review the details of the assets you have designated to be a part of your legacy and make sure that you aren't unintentionally disinheriting your heirs.
- Life insurance provides the distribution of tax-free, liquid assets to your beneficiaries.
- Investing in a life insurance policy can significantly build your legacy.
- Organizing your estate will allow you to make sure your wishes are properly carried through.
- You can take advantage of a "Stretch IRA" to provide income for you, your spouse and your beneficiaries throughout their lifetimes.
- Understand if your assets will be distributed *per stirpes* or *per capita*.
- Working with a financial professional can help you select the policy that best meets your needs, or can help you fine tune your existing policy to better reflect your desires and intentions.

15
HOW TO CHOOSE YOUR FINANCIAL PROFESSIONAL

From the moment you dip your toes into the retirement planning pool to the point you start swimming laps, your assets organized, your income needs met, and your accumulation and legacy plans in place, working with a professional that you trust can make all the difference in how well your retirement reflects your desires.

It is important to know what you are looking for before taking the plunge. There are many people that would love to handle your money, but not everyone is qualified to handle it in a way that leads to a holistic approach to creating a solid retirement plan.

The distinction being made here is that you should look for someone that puts your interests first and actively wants to help you meet your goals and objectives. Oftentimes, the products someone sells you matter less than their dedication to making sure that you have a plan that meets your needs.

Professionals take your whole financial position into consideration. They make plans that adjust your risk exposure, invest in tools that secure your desired income during retirement and create investment strategies that allow you to continue accumulating wealth during your retirement for you to use later or to contribute to your legacy. If you buy stocks with a broker, use

a different agent for a life insurance policy and have an unmanaged 401(k) through your employer, working with a financial professional will consolidate the management of your assets so you have one trustworthy person quarterbacking all of the team elements of your portfolio. Financial products and investment tools change, but the concepts that lie behind wise retirement planning are lasting. In the end, a financial professional's approach is designed for those serious about planning for retirement. *Can you say the same thing about the person that advises you about your financial life?*

It's easy to see how choosing a financial professional can be one of the most important decisions you can make in your life. Not only do they provide you with advice, they also manage the personal assets that supply your retirement income and contribute to your legacy. So, how do you find a good one?

HOW TO FIND A FINANCIAL PROFESSIONAL YOU CAN TRUST

Taking care to select a financial professional is one of the best things you can do for yourself and for your future. Your professional has influence and control of your investment decisions, making their role in your life more than just important. Your financial security and the quality of your retirement depends on the decisions, investment strategies and asset structuring that you and your professional create.

Working with a professional is different than calling up a broker when you want to buy or trade some stock. This isn't a decision that you can hand off to anyone else. You need to bring your time and attention to the table when it comes to finding someone with whom you can entrust your financial life. Separating the wheat from the chaff will take some work, but you'll be happy you did it.

While no one can tell you exactly who to choose or how to choose them, the following information can help you narrow the field:

- You can start by asking your friends, family and colleagues for referrals. You will want to pay particular attention to the recommendations that you get from others who are in your similar financial situation and who have similar lifestyle choices. The professional for the CEO of your company may have a different skill-set than the skill-set of the professional befitting your cousin who has 3 kids and a Subaru like you. Do follow-up research on the Internet as well. Look up the people who have been recommended to you on websites like LinkedIn that show the work history, referrals and experience of the candidates that you find most attractive. You will also learn about the firms with or for whom they work. The investment philosophies and reputations of the companies they work for will tell you a lot about how they will handle your money.
- The other side of the coin, however, is that everyone and their brother has a recommendation about how you should manage your money and who should manage it for you. From hot stock tips to "the best money manager in the state," people love to share good information that makes them look like they are in-the-know. Nobody wants to talk about the bad stock purchases they made, the times they lost money and the poor selections they made regarding financial professionals or stock brokers.

If you decide to take a friend or family member's recommendation, make sure they have a substantial, long-term experience with the financial professional and that their glowing review isn't just based on a one-time "win."
- You can also use online tools like the search function of the Financial Planning Association (http://www.fpanet. org/) and the National Association of Personal Financial professionals (http://www.napfa.org/). Most of the professionals listed on these sites do not earn commissions from selling financial products, but are instead paid on a fee-only basis for their services. It is important to understand how your professional is being paid. It is generally considered preferable to work with a fee-based professional who will not have conflicts of interests between earning a commission and acting in your best interests.
- Many professionals may also be brokers or dealers that can earn commissions on things like life insurance, certain types of annuities and disability insurance. These professionals have most likely intentionally overlapped their roles so that if their clients choose to purchase insurance or investment products that require a broker or dealer, those clients won't have to find an additional person to work with. Again, understanding the role of your professional will help you make your determination.

NARROWING THE FIELD
1. Decide on the Type of Professional with Whom You Want to Work. There are four basic kinds of financial professionals. Many professionals may play overlapping roles. It is important to know a professional's primary function, how they charge for their services and whether they are obligated to act in your best interest.

Registered representatives, better known as stockbrokers or bank/investment representatives, make their living by earning commissions on insurance products and investment services. Stockbrokers basically sell you things. The products from which they make the highest commission are sometimes the products that they recommend to their clients. If you want to make a simple transaction, such as buying or selling a particular stock, a registered representative can help you. Although registered representatives are licensed professionals, if you want to create a structured and planful approach to positioning your assets for retirement, you might want to consider continuing your search.

The term "planner" is often misused. A wide array of people may claim to be planners because there are no requirements to be a planner. The term financial planner, however, refers to someone who is properly registered as an investment advisor and serves as a fiduciary as described below.

Financial professionals are the diamonds in the rough. These Registered Investment Advisors are compensated on a fee basis. They do, however, often have licensure as stockbrokers or insurance agents, allowing them to earn commissions on certain transactions. More importantly, financial professionals are financial fiduciaries, meaning they are required to make financial decisions in your best interest and reflecting your risk tolerance. Investment Advisors are held to high ethical standards and are highly regarded in the financial industry. Financial professionals also often take a more comprehensive approach to asset management. These professionals are trained and credentialed to plan and coordinate their clients' assets in order to meet their goals or retirement and legacy planning. They are not focused on individual stocks, investments or markets. They look at the big picture, the whole enchilada.

Money managers are on par with financial professionals. However, they are often given explicit permission to make investment decisions without advanced approval by their clients.

Understanding who you are working with and what their title is the first step to planning your retirement. While each of the above-mentioned types of financial professionals can help you with aspects of your finances, it is financial professionals who have the most intimate role, the most objective investment strategies and the most unbiased mode of compensation for their services. A financial professional can also help you with the non-financial aspects of your legacy and can help you find ways to create a tax planning strategy to help you save money.

2. Be Objective. At the end of the day, you need to separate the weak from the strong. While you might want a strong personal rapport with your professional, or you may want to choose your professional for their personality and positive attitude, it is more important that you find someone who will give sage advice regarding achieving your retirement goals.

It can be helpful to use a process of elimination to narrow the field of potential professionals. Look into five or six potential leads and cross off your list the ones that don't meet your requirements until only one or two remain. Cross-check your remaining choices against the list of things you need from a professional. Make sure they represent a firm that has the investment tools and products that you desire, and make sure they have experience in retirement planning. That is, after all, the main goal.

Don't be afraid to investigate each of your candidates. You'll want to ask the same questions and look for the same information from everyone you consider so you can then compare them and discern which is best for you. You'll want to take a look at the specific credentials of each professional, their experience and competence, their ethics and fiduciary status, their history and track record, and a list of the services that they offer. The professionals who meet all or most of your qualifications are the ones you will contact for an interview.

Potential professionals should meet your qualifications in the following categories:

- *Credentials:* Look at their experience, the quality of their education, any associations to which they belong and certifications they have earned. Someone who has continued their professional education through ongoing certifications will be more up-to-date on current financial practices compared to someone who got their degree 25 years ago and hasn't done a thing since.
- *Practices:* Look at the track record of your candidates, how they are compensated for their services, the reports and analysis they offer, and their value added services.
- *Services:* Your professional must meet your needs. If you are planning your retirement, you should work with someone who offers services that help you to that end. You want someone who can offer planning, advice on investment strategies, ways to calculate risk, advice on insurance and annuities products, and ways to manage your tax strategy.
- *Ethics:* You want to work with someone who is above board and does things the right way. Vet them by checking their compliance record, current licensing, fiduciary status and, yes, even their criminal record. You never know!

3. Ask for and Check References. Once you have selected two or three professionals that you want to meet, call or email them and ask for references. Every professional should be able to provide you with at least two or three names. In fact, they will probably be eager to share them with you. Most professionals rely on references for validation of their success, quality of services and likability. You should, however, take them with a grain of salt. You have no way to know whether or not references are a professional's friends or colleagues.

It is worth contacting references, however, to check for inconsistencies. Ask each reference the same set of questions to get the same basic information. How long have they been working with the professional? What kind of services have they used and were they happy with them? What type of financial planning did they use the professional for? Were they versed in the type of financial planning that you needed? You can also ask them direct questions to elicit candid responses. What was the full cost of the expenses that your professional charged you? Do the reports and statements you receive come from the same firm? Questions like these can help you get a sense of how well the reference knows their professional and whether or not they are a quality reference.

A good reference is a bit like icing on the cake. It's nice to have them, but nothing speaks louder than a good track record and quality experience. And remember that a good reference, while nice to hear, is relatively cheap. How many times have you heard someone on the golf course or at work telling you how great their stockbroker is? But how many times have you heard about the bad investments or losses they have experienced?

4. Use the Internet. As a final step before picking up the phone and calling your candidates, do some digging to discover if anyone on your list has a history of unlawful or unethical practices, or has been disciplined for any of their professional behavior or decisions. Don't worry, you don't have to hire a private investigator. You can easily find this information on the Financial Industry Regulatory Authority's (FINRA) online BrokerCheck tool: http://www.finra.org/Investors/ToolsCalculators/BrokerCheck/.

You should obviously explore the website of a potential professional and the website of the firm that they represent. The Internet allows you to go beyond the online business card of a professional to gain access to information that they don't control. It may all be good information! Or a brief search of the Internet could reveal a sketchy past. The best part is that the Internet allows you to find helpful information in an anonymous fashion.

Start with Google (www.google.com) and search the name of a potential professional and their firm. Keep your eyes trained on third party sources such as articles, blog posts or news stories that mention the professional. You can also check a professional's compliance records online with the Financial Industry Regulatory Authority (FINRA) and the Securities and Exchange Commission (SEC).

HOW TO INTERVIEW CANDIDATES

After vetting your candidates and narrowing down a list of professionals that you think might be a good fit for you, it's time to start interviewing.

When you meet in person with an professional, you want to take advantage of your time with them. The presentations and information that they share with you will be important to pay attention to, but you will also want to control some aspects of the interview. After a professional has told you what they want you to hear, it's time to ask your own questions to get the specific information you need to make your decision.

Make sure to prepare a list of questions and an informal agenda so that you can keep track of what you want to ask and what points you want the professional to touch on during the interview. Using the same questions and agenda will also allow you to more easily compare the professionals after you have interviewed them all. Remember that these interviews are just that, *interviews*. Meeting with several professionals to determine with whom you want to work. Don't agree to anything or sign anything during an interview until after you have made your final decision.

It can also be helpful to put a time limit on your interviews and to meet the professionals at their offices. The time limit will keep things on track and will allow structured time for presentations and questions/discussion. By meeting them at their office, you can get a sense of the work environment, the staff culture and attitude, and how the firm does business. If you are unable to travel to a professional's office and must meet them at your home or office, make sure that your interviews are scheduled with plenty of time between so the professionals don't cross each other's paths.

You can use the following questions during an initial interview to get an understanding of how each professional does business and whether they are a good fit for you:

1. How do you charge for your services? How much do you charge? This information should be easy to find on their website, but if you don't see it, ask. Find out if they charge an initial planning fee, if they charge a percentage for assets under their management and if they make money by selling specific financial products or services. If so, you should follow up by asking how much the service costs. This will give you an idea of how they really make their money and if they have incentive to sell certain products over others. Make sure you understand exactly how you will be charged so there are no surprises down the road if you decide to work with this person.

2. What are the financial services that you and your firm provide? The question within the question here is, "Can you help me achieve my goals?" Some people can only provide you with investment advice, and others are tax consultants. You will likely want to work with someone that provides a complete suite of financial planning services and products that touch on retirement planning, insurance options, legacy and estate structuring, and tax planning. Whatever services they provide, make sure they meet your needs and your anticipated needs.

3. What kinds of clients do you work with the most? A lot of financial professionals work within a niche: retirement planning, risk assessment, life insurance, etc. Finding someone who works with other people that are in the same financial boat as you and who have similar goals can be an important way to make sure they understand your needs. While someone might be a crackerjack annuities cowboy, you might not be interested in that option. Ask follow-up questions that will really help you understand where their expertise lies and whether or not their experience lines up with your needs.

4. May I see a sample of one of your financial plans? You wouldn't buy a car without test driving it, and you should not work with a professional without seeing a sample of how they do business. While there is no formal structure that a financial plan has to follow, the variation between professionals can help you find someone who "speaks your language." One professional may provide you with an in-depth analysis that relies heavily on info graphics and diagrams. Someone else may give you a seven page review of your assets and general recommendations. By seeing a sample plan, you can narrow down who presents information in the way that you desire and in ways that you understand.

5. How do you approach investing? You may be entirely in the dark about how to approach your investments, or you might have some guiding principles. Either way, ask each candidate what their philosophy is. Some will resonate with you and some won't. A good professional who has a realistic approach to investing won't promise you the moon or tell you that they can make you a lot of money. Professionals who are successful at retirement planning and full service financial management will tell you that they will listen to your goals, risk tolerance and comfort level with different types of investment strategies. Working with someone that you trust is critical, and this question in particular can help you find out who you can and who you can't.

6. How do you remain in contact with your clients? Does your prospective professional hold annual, quarterly or monthly meetings? How often do *you* want to meet with your professional? Some people want to check in once a year, go over everything and make sure their ducks are all in a row. If any changes over the previous year or additions to their legacy planning strategy came up, they'll do it on that date. Other people want a monthly update to be more involved in the decision making process and to understand what's happening with their portfolio. You basically need to determine the right degree of involvement for both you and your financial professional. You'll also want to feel out how your professional communicates. Do you prefer phone calls or face-to-face meetings? Do you want your professional to explain things to you in detail or to summarize for you what decisions they've made? Is the professional willing to give you their direct phone number or their email address? More importantly, do you want that information and do you want to be able to contact them in those ways?

7. Are you my main contact, or do you work with a team? This is another way of finding out how involved with you your professional will be, and how often they will meet with you. It is also a way to discover how the firm they represent operates and manages their clients. Some professionals will answer their own phone, meet with you regularly and have your home phone number on speed dial. Others will meet with you once a year and have a partner or assistant check in with you every quarter to give you an update. Other companies take an entirely team-based approach whereby clients have a main contact but their portfolio is handled by a team of professionals that represent the firm. One way isn't better than another, but one way will be best for you. Find out how the professional you are interviewing operates before entering into an agreement.

8. How do you provide a unique experience for your clients? This is a polite way of asking, "Why should I work with you?" A professional should have a compelling answer to this question that connects with you. Their answer will likely touch on their investment philosophy, their communication style and their expertise. If you hear them describing strengths and philosophies that resonate with you, keep them on your list. Some professionals will tell you that they will make investments with your money that match your values, others will say they will maximize your returns and others will say they will protect your capital while structuring your assets for income. Whatever you're looking for in a professional, you will most likely find it in the answer to this question.

This last question you will want to ask *yourself* after you've met with someone who you are considering hiring:

9. Did they ask questions and show signs that they were interested in working with me? A professional who will structure your assets to reflect your risk tolerance and to position you for a comfortable retirement must be a good listener. You will want to pass by a professional who talks non-stop and tells you what to do without listening to what you want them to do. If you felt they listened well and understood your needs, and seemed interested and experienced in your situation, then they might be right for you.

THE IMPORTANCE OF INDEPENDENCE

Not all investment firms and financial professionals are created equal. The information in this book has systematically shown that leveraging investments for income and accumulation in today's market requires new ideas and modern planning. In short, you need innovative ideas to come up with the creative solutions that will provide you with the retirement that you want. Innovation thrives on independence. No matter how good a financial professional is, the firm that they represent needs to operate on principles that make sense in today's economy. Remember, advice about money has been around forever. Good advice, however, changes with the times.

Timing the market, relying on the sale of stocks for income and banking on high treasury and bond returns are not strategies. They aren't even realistic ways to make money or to generate income. Working with an independent advisor can help you break free from the old ways of thinking and position you to create a realistic retirement plan.

Working with an independent advisor who relies on fee-based income tied to the success of their performance will also give you greater peace of mind. When you do well, they do well, and that's the way it should be. Your independent advisor will make sure that:

- Your assets are organized and structured to reflect your risk tolerance.
- Your assets will be available to you when you need them and in the way that you need them.
- You will have a lifetime income that will support your lifestyle through your retirement.
- You are handling your taxes as efficiently as possible.
- Your legacy is in order.
- Your Red Money is turned into Yellow Money, and is managed in your best interest.

» *Remember Florence and Raymond from Chapter 1? Even though they knew they had Social Security benefits coming, they placed some money in savings and each had a pension or a*

401(k). **Before they met with a financial professional, they had no idea what their retirement would look like.** *After they met with an agent, they knew exactly what types of assets they had, how much they were worth, how much risk they were exposed to and how they were going to be distributed. They also created an income plan so that they could pay their bills every month the moment they retired, and they maximized their Social Security benefit by targeting the year and month they would get the most lifetime benefits. After their income needs were met, they were able to continue accumulating wealth by investing their extra assets to serve them in the future and contribute to their legacy. Their professional also helped them make decisions that impacted their taxes, protecting the value of their assets and allowing them to keep more of their money.*

*This isn't a fairy tale scenario. This is an example of how much you stand to gain by meeting with a financial professional who can help you create a planful approach to your retirement. The concept of Know So and Hope So didn't just apply to their money, it also applied to Florence and Raymond. They **hoped** that they would have enough for retirement and that they had worked hard enough and saved enough to maintain their lifestyle. Working with a financial professional allowed them to **know** that their income needs were secured and structured to provide them with income for the rest of their lives and with some money to spare.*

Now, ask yourself: Is your retirement built on hopes and dreams, or a solid, predictable plan?

IT'S WORTH IT!

Finding, interviewing and selecting a financial professional can seem like a daunting task. And honestly, it will take a good amount of work to narrow the field and find the one you want. In the end, it is worth the blood, sweat and tears. Your retirement, lifestyle, assets and legacy is on the line. The choices you make today will have lasting impacts on your life and the life of your loved ones. Working with someone you trust and know you can rely on to make decisions that will benefit you is invaluable. The work it takes to find them is something you will never regret.

Here is a recap of why working with a financial professional is the best retirement decision you can make:

CHAPTER 15 RECAP //

- If you feel you have more *Hope So* than *Know So* about your money and what your retirement is going to look like, working with a financial professional will give you clarity and confidence about what decisions are best for you.
- It is difficult for individual investors to not make emotional decisions about their investments. Financial professionals work with your risk tolerance, income needs and assets to find the most logical, efficient and beneficial way for you to structure your investments.
- As the DALBAR report showed, a majority of individual investors sell low when the market goes down and buy high when it goes back up. This is literally the exact opposite of what they should do to maximize their returns. Why? Emotions.
- A financial professional can help you change strategies when the market isn't going your way, but they won't abandon ship. They will stick to a planful approach. Your retirement isn't based on individual products or investments. It is based on a well-planned strategy that your financial professional is qualified to provide.
- Yellow Money is different from a mutual fund or a 401(k) because, while funds and 401(k)s are investment tools,

HOW TO CHOOSE YOUR FINANCIAL PROFESSIONAL

they are not investment strategies. A 401(k) can be particularly misconceiving because your employer isn't truly structuring your investments inside the 401(k). They are simply providing you with a few options. The same goes for mutual funds. They are not truly managed by someone who is obligated to have your best interests and your risk tolerance in mind. In fact, the investment strategies of mutual funds change on a regular basis, and you might not know about it until you get an annual report a *month* later.

- The biggest difference between working with a financial professional to manage your funds, and buying a mutual fund is that, while a mutual fund buys 20 stocks and pegs its earnings on the overall performance of the portfolio, a financial professional works with you to create an overall financial strategy that meets your needs. It may or may not include mutual funds.
- As an individual investor, do you really have an overarching strategy for your financial portfolio? How did you come up with your selections? Do you know how they are individually managed? Do you know how to make changes to your portfolio that reflect your risk tolerance? Do you know what your risk tolerance is?
- Managed money has a specific criteria and a professional will fit that into your overall financial plan so that it works the way you want it to.
- Not all investment firms and financial professionals are created equal. Working with an independent professional will give you more options that are customizable to your life.

GLOSSARY

ANNUAL RESET *(ANNUAL RATCHET, CLIQUET)* – Crediting methods measuring index movement over a one year period. Positive interest is calculated and credited at the end of each contract year and cannot be lost if the index subsequently declines. Say that the index increased from 100 to 110 in one year and the indexed annuity had an 80 percent participation rate. The insurance company would take the 10 percent gross index gain for the year (110-100/100), apply the participation rate (10 percent index gain x 80 percent rate) and credit 8 percent interest to the annuity. But, what if in the following year the index declined back to 100? The individual would keep the 8 percent interest earned and simply receive zero interest for the down year. An annual reset structure preserves credited gains and treats negative index periods as years with zero growth.

ANNUITANT – The person, usually the annuity owner, whose life expectancy is used to calculate the income payment amount on the annuity.

GLOSSARY

ANNUITY – An annuity is a contract issued by an insurance company that often serves as a type of savings plan used by individuals looking for long term growth and protection of assets that will likely be needed within retirement.

AVERAGING – Index values may either be measured from a start point to an end point (point-to-point) or values between the start point and end point may be averaged to determine an ending value. Index values may be averaged over the days, weeks, months or quarters of the period.

BENEFICIARY – A beneficiary is the person designated to receive payments due upon the death of the annuity owner or the annuitant themselves.

BONUS RATE – A bonus rate is the "extra" or "additional" interest paid during the first year (the initial guarantee period), typically used as an added incentive to get consumers to select their annuity policy over another.

CALL OPTION *(ALSO SEE PUT OPTION)* – Gives the holder the right to buy an underlying security or index at a specified price on or before a given date.

CAP – The maximum interest rate that will be credited to the annuity for the year or period. The cap usually refers to the maximum interest credited after applying the participation rate or yield spread. If the index methodology showed a 20 percent increase, the participation rate was 60 percent and the maximum interest cap was 10 percent, the contract would credit 10 percent interest. A few annuities use a maximum gain cap instead of a maximum interest cap with the participation rate or yield spread applied to the lesser of the gain or the cap. If the index methodology showed a 20 percent increase, the participation rate was 60 percent and the maximum gain cap was 10 percent, the contract would credit 6 percent interest.

COMPOUND INTEREST – Interest is earned on both the original principal and on previously earned interest. It is more favorable than simple interest. Suppose that your original principal was $1 and your interest rate was 10 percent for five years. With simple interest, your value is ($1 + $0.10 interest each year) = $1.50. With compound interest, your value is ($1 x 1.10 x 1.10 x 1.10 x 1.10 x 1.10) = $1.61. The advantage of compound interest over simple interest becomes greater as each subsequent period passes.

CREDITING METHOD *(ALSO SEE METHODOLOGY)* – The formula(s) used to determine the excess interest that is credited above the minimum interest guarantee.

DEATH BENEFITS – The payment the annuity owner's estate or beneficiaries will receive if he or she dies before the annuity matures. On most annuities, this is equal to the current account value. Some annuities offer an enhanced value at death via an optional rider that has a monthly or annual fee associated with it.

EXCESS INTEREST – Interest credited to the annuity contract above the minimum guaranteed interest rate. In an indexed annuity the excess interest is determined by applying a stated crediting method to a specific index or indices.

FIXED ANNUITY – A contract issued by an insurance company guaranteeing a minimum interest rate with the crediting of excess interest determined by the performance of the insurer's general account. Index annuities are fixed annuities.

GLOSSARY

FIXED DEFERRED ANNUITY – With fixed annuities, an insurance company offers a guaranteed interest rate plus safety of your principal and earnings ((subject to the claims-paying ability of the insurance company). Your interest rate will be reset periodically, based on economic and other factors, but is guaranteed to never fall below a certain rate.

FREE WITHDRAWALS – Withdrawals that are free of surrender charges.

INDEX – The underlying external benchmark upon which the crediting of excess interest is based, also a measure of the prices of a group of securities.

IRA *(INDIVIDUAL RETIREMENT ACCOUNT)* – An IRA is a tax-advantaged personal savings plan that lets an individual set aside money for retirement. All or part of the participant's contributions may be tax deductible, depending on the type of IRA chosen and the participant's personal financial circumstances. Distributions from many employer-sponsored retirement plans may be eligible to be rolled into an IRA to continue tax-deferred growth until the funds are needed. An annuity can be used as an IRA; that is, IRA funds can be used to purchase an annuity.

IRA ROLLOVER – IRA rollover is the phrase used when an individual who has a balance in an employer-sponsored retirement plan transfers that balance into an IRA. Such an exchange, when properly handled, is a tax-advantaged transaction.

LIQUIDITY – The ease with which an asset is convertible to cash. An asset with high liquidity provides flexibility, in that the owner can easily convert it to cash at any time, but it also tends to decrease profitability.

MARKET RISK – The risk of the market value of an asset fluctuating up or down over time. In a fixed or fixed indexed annuity, the original principal and credited interest are not subject to market risk. Even if the index declines, the annuity owner would receive no less than their original principal back if they decided to cash in the policy at the end of the surrender period. Unlike a security, indexed annuities guarantee the original premium and the premium is backed by, and is as safe as, the insurance company that issued it (subject to the claims-paying ability of the insurance company).

METHODOLOGY *(ALSO SEE CREDITING METHOD)* – The way that interest crediting is calculated. On fixed indexed annuities, there are a variety of different methods used to determine how index movement becomes interest credited.

MINIMUM GUARANTEED RETURN *(MINIMUM INTEREST RATE)* – Fixed indexed annuities typically provide a minimum guaranteed return over the life of the contract. At the time that the owner chooses to terminate the contract, the cash surrender value is compared to a second value calculated using the minimum guaranteed return and the higher of the two values is paid to the annuity owner.

OPTION – A contract which conveys to its holder the right, but not the obligation, to buy or sell something at a specified price on or before a given date. After this given date the option ceases to exist. Insurers typically buy options to provide for the excess interest potential. Options may be American style whereby they may be exercised at any time prior to the given date, or they may have to be exercised only during a specified window. Options that may only be exercised during a specified period are European-style options.

OPTION RISK – Most insurers create the potential for excess interest in an indexed annuity by buying options. Say that you

GLOSSARY

could buy a share of stock for $50. If you bought the stock and it rose to $60 you could sell it and net a $10 profit. But, if the stock price fell to $40 you'd have a $10 loss. Instead of buying the actual stock, we could buy an option that gave us the right to buy the stock for $50 at any time over the next year. The cost of the option is $2. If the stock price rose to $60 we would exercise our option, buy the stock at $50 and make $10 (less the $2 cost of the option). If the price of the stock fell to $40, $30 or $10, we wouldn't use the option and it would expire. The loss is limited to $2 – the cost of the option.

PARTICIPATION RATE – The percentage of positive index movement credited to the annuity. If the index methodology determined that the index increased 10 percent and the indexed annuity participated in 60 percent of the increase, it would be said that the contract has a 60 percent participation rate. Participation rates may also be expressed as asset fees or yield spreads.

POINT-TO-POINT – A crediting method measuring index movement from an absolute initial point to the absolute end point for a period. An index had a period starting value of 100 and a period ending value of 120. A point-to-point method would record a positive index movement of 20 [120-100] or a 20 percent positive movement [(120-100)/100]. Point-to-point usually refers to annual periods; however the phrase is also used instead of term end point to refer to multiple year periods.

PREMIUM BONUS – A premium bonus is additional money that is credited to the accumulation account of an annuity policy under certain conditions.

PUT OPTION *(ALSO SEE CALL OPTION)* – Gives the holder the right to sell an underlying security or index at a specified price on or before a given date.

QUALIFIED ANNUITIES *(QUALIFIED MONEY)* – Qualified annuities are annuities purchased for funding an IRA, 403(b) tax-deferred annuity or other type of retirement arrangements. An IRA or qualified retirement plan provides the tax deferral. An annuity contract should be used to fund an IRA or qualified retirement plan to benefit from an annuity's features other than tax deferral, including the safety features, lifetime income payout option and death benefit protection.

REQUIRED MINIMUM DISTRIBUTION *(RMD)* – The amount of money that Traditional, SEP and SIMPLE IRA owners and qualified plan participants must begin distributing from their retirement accounts by April 1 following the year they reach age 70.5. RMD amounts must then be distributed each subsequent year.

RETURN FLOOR – Another way of saying minimum guaranteed return.

ROTH IRA – Like other IRA accounts, the Roth IRA is simply a holding account that manages your stocks, bonds, annuities, mutual funds and CD's. However, future withdrawals (including earnings and interest) are typically tax-advantaged once the account has been open for five years and the account holder is age 59.5.

RULE OF 72 – Tells you approximately how many years it takes a sum to double at a given rate. It's handy to be able to figure out, without using a calculator, that when you're earning a 6 percent return, for example, by dividing 6 percent into 72, you'll find that it takes 12 years for money to double. Conversely, if you know it took a sum twelve years to double you could divide 12 into 72 to determine the annual return (6 percent).

GLOSSARY

SIMPLE INTEREST *(ALSO SEE COMPOUND INTEREST)* – Interest is only earned on the original principal.

SPLIT ANNUITY – A split annuity is the term given to an effective strategy that utilizes two or more different annuity products – one designed to generate monthly income and the other to restore the original starting principal over a set period of time.

STANDARD & POOR'S 500 *(S&P 500)* – The most widely used external index by fixed indexed annuities. Its objective is to be a benchmark to measure and report overall U.S. stock market performance. It includes a representative sample of 500 common stocks from companies trading on the New York Stock Exchange, American Stock Exchange, and NASDAQ National Market System. The index represents the price or market value of the underlying stocks and does not include the value of reinvested dividends of the underlying stocks.

STOCK MARKET INDEX – A report created from a type of statistical measurement that shows up or down changes in a specific financial market, usually expressed as points and as a percentage, in a number of related markets, or in an economy as a whole (i.e. S&P 500 or New York Stock Exchange).

SURRENDER CHARGE – A charge imposed for withdrawing funds or terminating an annuity contract prematurely. There is no industry standard for surrender charges, that is, each annuity product has its own unique surrender charge schedule. The charge is usually expressed as a percentage of the amount withdrawn prematurely from the contract. The percentage tends to decline over time, ultimately becoming zero.

TRADITIONAL IRA – See IRA (Individual Retirement Account)

TERM END POINT – Crediting methods measuring index movements over a greater timeframe than a year or two. The opposite of an annual reset method. Also referred to as a term point-to-point method. Say that the index value was at 100 on the first day of the period. If the calculated index value was at 150 at the end of the period the positive index movement would be 50 percent (150-100/100). The company would credit a percentage of this movement as excess interest. Index movement is calculated and interest credited at the end of the term and interim movements during the period are ignored.

TERM HIGH POINT *(HIGH WATER MARK)* – A type of term end point structure that uses the highest anniversary index level as the end point. Say that the index value was at 100 on the first day of the period, reached a value of 160 at the end of a contract year during the period, and ended the period at 150. A term high point method would use the 160 value – the highest contract anniversary point reached during the period, as the end point and the gross index gain would be 60 percent (160-100/100). The company would then apply a participation rate to the gain.

TERM YIELD SPREAD – A type of term end point structure which calculates the total index gain for a period, computes the annual compound rate of return deducts a yield spread from the annual rate of return and then recalculates the total index gain for the period based on the net annual rate. Say that an index increased from 100 to 200 by the end of a nine year period. This is the equivalent of an 8 percent compound annual interest rate. If the annuity had a 2 percent term yield spread this would be deducted from the annual interest rate (8 percent-2 percent) and the net rate would be credited to the contract (6 percent) for each of the nine years. Total index gain may also be computed by using the highest anniversary index level as the end point.

VARIABLE ANNUITY – A contract issued by an insurance company offering separate accounts invested in a wide variety of stocks and/or bonds. The investment risk is borne by the annuity owner. Variable annuities are considered securities and require appropriate securities registration.

1035 EXCHANGE – The 1035 exchange refers to the section of tax code that allows annuity owners the flexibility to exchange one annuity for another without incurring any immediate tax liabilities. This action is most often utilized when an annuity holder decides they want to upgrade an annuity to a more favorable one, but they do not want to activate unnecessary tax liabilities that would typically be encountered when surrendering an existing annuity contract.

401(K) ROLLOVER – See IRA Rollover

13318705R00108

Made in the USA
San Bernardino, CA
19 July 2014

Made in the USA
San Bernardino, CA
19 July 2014